THE
LITTLE
BOOK
OF
SANDYMOUNT

KURT KULLMANN

The
History
Press

Dedicated to the Donovan family of Wilfield Road

First published 2016

This paperback edition published 2022

The History Press
97 St George's Place, Cheltenham,
Gloucestershire, GL50 3QB
www.thehistorypress.co.uk

British Library Cataloguing in Publication Data.
A catalogue record for this book is available from the British Library.

ISBN 978 1 80399 125 2

Typesetting and origination by The History Press
Printed and bound in Great Britain by TJ Books Limited, Padstow,
Cornwall.

CONTENTS

ACKNOWLEDGMENTS

I am grateful to very many people who have helped with this book. First of all, I have to mention the Donovan family, who have lived in Sandymount since 1944 and whom I have known since 1971. Many facts and incidents described were mentioned in discussions and conversations with members of this family, especially my late father-in-law John Donovan and, of course, my wife Catherine. Living in Sandymount myself for the last seventeen years, I have met many Sandymount people who had lots of stories to tell. A great thank you goes to the Siggins family, Brian in the first place, but also his brother David and his son Gerard. Mary O'Neill, the parish secretary of the Star of the Sea, and Revd Katherine Meyer of Christ Church, Sandymount, are among the people who might not even remember helping me. Among my neighbours, it was especially the late Malachy Ryan and Francis X. Carty who provided information, the latter sharing a lot of his knowledge of sport. Many more people have helped. I cannot name them all, but I am nonetheless very grateful to all of them.

FOREWORD

My earliest memory of Sandymount is when, jointly with my cousin T.P. McCurtain from Lea Road, I won third place in the Sandymount Strand sandcastle competition. I was about 6. He went on to be a successful artist and I retained my love for this incredibly beautiful part of Dublin. Like so many Dublin children, I remember many trips to the beach, with my mother packing up the towels and swimming togs, the Mi-Wadi orange, the wrapped-up sandwiches and then the walk down from our home in Donnybrook. I remember also the large, bold, white-painted letters, 'SAVE OUR STRAND', on the old baths, though I did not know at the time that this was part of a campaign by people such as the late Jack Torpey and Harry Mapother and the Sandymount and Merrion Residents Association (SAMRA) to protect this incredible resource.

We owe so much to them and all their successors, such as Lorna Kelly, Michael McAuliffe, Tony Reid and the late Catherine Cavendish, who have done so much to protect the village and the strand. It is not their fault that over the years city and national figures have abused this wonderful natural amenity. The struggle to reverse the effects of such damaging interventions must go on.

But Sandymount is much more than the strand. It is more than the Green, more than the Nature Park and more than its vibrant and rich history – a history so richly recorded by people such as Brian Siggins, the late Kevin O'Rorke, Hugh Oram and now Kurt Kullmann. Sandymount is one of the great villages of Dublin. It really does have it all: location, heritage, environment, culture, elegance and style. But above all, it has a wonderful, committed, diverse and inclusive community.

For many years, I have had the honour of representing Sandymount on Dublin City Council and I am grateful to the people of the area for giving me their trust. But more than that, I am grateful for their friendship, for their enthusiasm, for the many great nights I have had during community weeks, the Sandymount, Irishtown and Ringsend Arts Festival (SIRAF), the Yeats celebrations and the Bloomsday events. I am grateful for the times spent with the late Frank Geoghegan, who led Sandymount Scouts, and Teresa Devlin, who led Roslyn Park Guides, and the many young people I came to know through them. The notion that I would spend St Stephen's Day anywhere other than at 'The Green' – with an occasional pint from Ryan's and O'Reilly's in hand – is alien to me. If 'the Wran was not being chased in Sandymount', I don't know what I would do.

I will forever be proud of the success of Sandymount Community Services that I co-founded with Ann Ingle at the instigation of Ruairi Quinn back in 1985. For nearly thirty years, SCS has published *News Four*, given hundreds of people an opportunity to work and, through Denis McKenna and his successors, produced a variety of publications of local interest.

Kurt Kullmann has now added to that volume of work, celebrating this community and recording its history, and it is a privilege and a challenge to write this foreword. As the world becomes a more global village, the importance of the real village, the true home place, the local community, will hopefully become even clearer. Knowing about our locality, about where we live, can only help us build living, thriving communities.

In this wonderful evocation of Sandymount, Kurt Kullmann has done more than help us achieve that; he has breathed new life into our past and inspired new hope for our collective future. I hope you enjoy reading it for the first time – for you will surely read it more than once as you will find yourself dipping back into it again and again, with greater pleasure each time.

Cllr Dermot Lacey, 2016

INTRODUCTION

Sandymount is one of the youngest of Dublin's suburbs and, as most inhabitants of Sandymount will agree, it is also one of the most pleasant ones: green and near the sea, yet not far from city centre, which can be reached quickly and easily by public transport. It is quiet in the sense that there is not really any industry, but its centre can grow quite lively in the evenings.

That is not to say that there are no disadvantages to living there, as commuters who do not rely on public transport will know. Finding a parking space in Sandymount on weekdays is not easy and those found are pay-and-display. To leave the village westwards by car, by bike or on foot can test your patience as you have to cross one of the five level crossings, the only level crossings on the old Dublin & Kingstown Railway line within the borders of Dublin City.

One point of dispute is the borders of Sandymount. Some even say that the postal address is 'Ballsbridge' as Ballsbridge has a post office and Sandymount has only ever had a sub-post office. Purists insist that only the townland named Sandymount should be regarded as Sandymount. That would mean that neither Sandymount DART station nor the Sandymount parish church of Our Lady Star of the Sea nor Sandymount Tower would be in Sandymount; the first would be in Ballsbridge (Smotscourt townland), the second in Irishtown and the third in Merrion townlands.

As far as this book is concerned, let us come to a compromise. We shall acknowledge a core village, an extended village and a very extended village. Both the core and extended village have the railway as the western and the sea as the eastern border. For the core village, the northern border runs along the Dodder, Newbridge Avenue, a part of Sandymount Road and Cranfield Place and the southern border is St John's and St John's Road. This is slightly bigger than Sandymount townland and includes the DART station, the parish church and the Martello tower. The extended village is what the Sandymount Village Design Statement of Dublin City Council regards as Sandymount. In this statement, the northern border runs along Bath Avenue, Londonbridge Road and Church Avenue and in the south Sandymount stretches out to Merrion Gates, where railway and sea come together. This includes a part of Irishtown in the north and all of Merrion east of the railway in the south as parts of Sandymount. The very extended village additionally includes all of Sandymount Avenue and Serpentine Avenue, even the parts west of the railway, so these two streets are in Sandymount for their whole length.

There could still be disagreement. For instance, if the sea is the eastern border of Sandymount, does that mean the high water mark or the low water mark? Let's regard the eastern border of Sandymount as a moveable feast; in other words, Sandymount stretches as far eastwards as you can walk without getting your feet wet. Any further complains should be addressed to Richard, 7th Viscount Fitzwilliam of Merrion and Baron Fitzwilliam of Thorncastle, as he invented the name 'Sandymount' for a village for which he did not draw borders.

1

HISTORY AND POLITICS

Sandymount might be one of the youngest suburban villages
of Dublin, but that does not mean that the area and the village
have no history.

TIMELINE

BCE

c. 4000	Mesolithic finds on Dublin Bay (Dalkey Island and Sutton) date to this period
c. 2000	Beginning of metal age; copper and gold from Wicklow Mountains are worked
c. 600	Portal tombs, wedge tombs and dolmens are built in the area
c. 400	La Tène culture and a Celtic language start to spread through Ireland

CE

431	The first definite date in Irish history: St Palladius is sent to Ireland
795	The first Fionnghall Viking attacks in Ireland
842	Vikings settle in Dubhlinn
c. 850	Dubhgall Vikings arrive
851–1171	The Viking kingdom of Dublin: Dyfflinarskiri
1014	The Battle of Clontarf
1171	The Siege of Dublin by Diarmait Mac Murchada with his Norman allies

1171	Ascall mac Torcaill, last Norse king of Dublin, is beheaded
1171	Walter de Ridelesford is granted lands from Ringsend to Bray
1238	Walter de Ridelesford (the younger) grants Simmonscourt to Frambald FitzBoydeken
1258	FitzBoydeken's son John Frambald leases Simmonscourt to Richard de St Olof
1334	The first mention of Merrion Castle
1536	The Reformation in Ireland
1629	Thomas Fitzwilliam is created Viscount Fitzwilliam of Merrion and Baron Fitzwilliam of Thorncastle
1661	Oliver, 2nd Viscount Fitzwilliam, is created Earl of Tyconnell
1710	Richard, 5th Viscount Fitzwilliam, converts to the Established Church
c. 1725	Conniving House is built
c. 1730–1785	Brick industry in 'Lord Merrion's Brickfields'
1789	Roslyn Park is built
1791	Sea wall is built
1816	George Augustus Herbert, 11th Earl of Pembroke, inherits the Fitzwilliam Estate
1831	The Sisters of Charity are called to Sandymount by Barbara Verschoyle
1833	The Schoolhouse on Sandymount Green is erected by subscription
1835	First railway stop for Sandymount
1837	The first ordnance survey map of the area is finished
1850	The first church in Sandymount, St John the Evangelist, is opened for worship
c. 1850	The first horse-drawn bus to Sandymount
1856	Discalced Carmelite Sisters move into Lakelands
1863	Pembroke Township is established
1864	Important cricket match between Sandymount Cricket Club and County Wicklow Cricket Club

1867	Pembroke Township is connected to Vartry water supply
1872	The first tramline to Sandymount opens, terminating at Sandymount Tower
1876	The Sisters of Charity move to Lakelands in exchange with the Carmelite Sisters
1876	Sandymount becomes a Roman Catholic parish
1898	Pembroke Township becomes an Urban District. Franchise extended for local elections
1901	Electrification of trams finished (line no. 4 to Sandymount the last to be electrified)
1930	Pembroke Urban District is incorporated into Dublin Corporation
1932	Tramline no. 4 is replaced by bus no. 52
1939–1945	'The Emergency', otherwise known as the Second World War
1940	Tramlines nos 2 and 3 are replaced by bus
1984	Dublin Area Rapid Transport (DART) starts service
2006	Lansdowne Road Stadium closes
2010	Aviva Stadium opens
2016	*The Little Book of Sandymount* published

PREHISTORY

According to the most recent research, the first human beings reached Ireland in the Palaeolithic period *c*. 12,000 years ago. At the end of the Mesolithic period, around 4000 BCE, more people came to Ireland, most likely from Scotland. Perhaps they were attracted by the slightly milder weather in Ireland, perhaps they were just curious and decided to go and see what was there as there was a land bridge between the two countries at the time. Since then, there has been constant comings and goings between Scotland and Ireland – and not only of soccer and rugby fans.

Some of those early people made it to Dalkey Island and left traces there. As they were known to have fished rivers and lakes, the marshy land with many pools and streams south of the Dodder and the Dodder itself would have been attractive for them. No artefacts have been found in this area, but the regular inundations by the sea or the Dodder, or both at the same time, mean that most likely no remains ever will be found.

The Stone Age was followed by the Bronze Age. Copper and gold can be found in the Wicklow Mountains and at least some of it might have been washed down by the Dodder. During the Bronze Age, weapon technology was greatly improved, leading to more effective warfare. This had an enormous and not always positive impact on the consequent history of Ireland.

The Iron Age that followed is usually associated with the arrival of Celtic art and a Celtic language. Today it is no longer thought that great masses of Celtic warriors invaded Ireland and settled here.

ST PALLADIUS

This early saint provides the east coast of Ireland with the first date that can be confirmed. In CE 431, one year before St Patrick arrived in Ireland, Palladius was sent to those Irish people who believed in Christ to be their first bishop. He landed on the east coast between the Liffey and Wicklow and is said to have converted some inhabitants. The rest of them, however, behaved so aggressively that he moved on from there to Scotland to Christianise the Picts. He had built some little churches on the Irish east coast though and commanded a couple of his companions to stay there. He left some books with them. As books were very valuable at that time, these early missionaries must have either found safe places for them or friendly inhabitants who protected them.

NORSE

It is possible that all these prehistoric and early historic peoples bypassed our area. The Vikings, however, did not. The Vikings, also called the Norse or the Ostmen, came by boat. Their boats had a minimal draught, so the many sandbanks in Dublin Bay did not worry them.

They used rivers to invade inland from the coast. We know they went up the Liffey, so why not the Dodder also? This would have been the easiest way for them to reach the monastery of St Máel Ruain in Tallaght. From the end of the eighth to the middle of the ninth century, they came frequently on short raids. In 842, they settled in Dublin and founded Dyfflinarskiri, a coastal kingdom which included the Sandymount area and had Dublin as capital. The surrounding Irish fought against them for the most part, but at times they also fought for them. Dyfflinarskiri did not have a peaceful history until the late tenth century, by which time the Norse and the Irish had intermarried and were learning to live with and among each other.

The Irish distinguished between two different groups of Norse. The first group, said to have come originally from Norway, were called Fionnghall, the white strangers. The second group, supposed to have been from Denmark, were called the dark strangers, Dubhghall. This later turned into

A Viking longship.

'Doyle', the second most common name in this area (after Byrne).

The Battle of Clontarf in 1014 is often described as a battle between the Irish under Brian Boru and the Vikings under Sihtric Silkbeard. This was not the case. It was a battle between Munster Irish and Limerick Vikings under Brian Boru and the Laighin Irish under Máel Mórda mac Murchada with his subjects, the Vikings of Dublin. Despite what very many people in Ireland think, the Vikings were not evicted from Ireland in this battle. The last Norse king of Dublin, Ascall mac Torcaill, also mentioned as Hasculf MacTurcail or Höskellr Thorkelson in Nordic, reigned in the second half of the twelfth century. He was beaten by the Normans in 1171. In that battle, he was taken captive and had to pay a high ransom to buy his freedom. He then boasted that he would come back with a much bigger army and beat the Normans. The Normans beheaded him there and then. It is unlikely that they paid back the ransom.

NORMANS

As a matter of fact, the Normans are Norse as well. Those Northmen just settled in a part of France opposite the south coast of England and changed their name slightly from Northman to Norman. They learnt to speak French instead of a Norse language, and then crossed the Channel and became rulers in England.

As it happened, one of the kings of the Laighin who had some disagreements with other Irish kings asked the Norman king of England for help. That brought the Normans into Ireland. The leader of those Normans, Richard FitzGilbert de Clare, better known as Strongbow, gave the coastal land from Dublin to Wicklow to his companion Walter de Ridelesford (or Riddleford) who is said to have killed John the Wode, one of the fiercest warriors of the Norse from the Isles, in that campaign.

After de Ridelesford's death, the land was passed on to his son, also called Walter de Ridelesford. The often cited 'fact' that Richard de St Olof was the first owner of Sandymount is not correct. At this time, Sandymount was part of the Simmonscourt Estate. In 1238, Walter de Ridelesford (the younger) granted Simmonscourt to Frambald FitzBoydeken, whose son John Frambald leased it to Richard de St Olof in 1258 for the rent of a pair of gloves, so Richard de St Olof became a tenant of the area more than eighty years after the de Ridelesfords became its owners.

THE FITZWILLIAMS ...

The land passed through several families' hands, including the Bagods, whose name is remembered in Baggot Street, and the Smothes, after whom the townlands Smotscourt and Simmonscourt are called. It finally came into the hands of the Fitzwilliams. The Fitzwilliams were of Norman origin and are supposed to have come to Ireland at the beginning of the thirteenth century in the time of King John. Between the fourteenth and the seventeenth centuries, the family managed to amass much land in this area, including the castles of Merrion, Thorncastle, Baggotrath and Dundrum, with their estates. They also had possessions in Bray in County Wicklow and in Holmpatrick in Fingal County.

There were some interesting characters in the long line of Fitzwilliams. In the fourteenth century, some were made Guardian of the Peace and Sheriff of County Dublin. Thomas Fitzwilliam (*c*. 1465–1517) was Sheriff of County Dublin in 1511, lived in Baggotrath Castle and owned the castles of Dundrum, Bray, Baggotrath, Merrion and Thorn Castle, as well as the lands of Booterstown, Mount Merrion, Kilmacud, Ballinteer, Donnybrook, Ringsend, Irishtown and Sandymount (except that it was not called Sandymount then). His son, Sir Thomas Fitzwilliam, was Vice-Treasurer of Ireland in 1559. Yet another Thomas Fitzwilliam (1581–*c*. 1655) was created Viscount Fitzwilliam of Merrion and Baron Fitzwilliam of Thorncastle in 1629 by King Charles I because of his family's long service to the Crown, despite the fact that the Fitzwilliams were Catholics. He was even allowed to take his seat in the Irish House of Lords in 1634.

Oliver, second son of Thomas, 1st Viscount, fought with the Royalist Confederates against the Parliamentarians. He went to France in the service of Henrietta, the French Queen Consort of Charles I. He was a strong enough force on the Confederate side to be referred to in a contemporary letter from the Parliamentarian side, quoted in Richard Cox's *History of Ireland*, 1689:

> The new Agent of the Supream Council, Colonel Fitz-Williams, is very violent in his office ... He, the Colonel, is very liberal in the disposing of Places and Offices in the Kingdom ... Colonel Fitz-Williams hath said in great heat, That Dublin should be taken as soon as Mr. Baron returned, and that the Confederates are so puissant that he wisheth with all his Heart that there were in Ireland 40,000 English and Scots, that they might have the Honour to beat them.

His service with the Confederates resulted in his incarceration after Cromwell's victory. He cannot be as wild as he was painted in the quoted letter as he was let out of prison under the condition that he leave the country. He went to France, where he had served before, but through the pleas of his brother-in-law, John Holles, Earl of Clare and a Parliamentarian, he was allowed to return. He was said to be one of the few Irishmen that Oliver Cromwell admired. Oliver Fitzwilliam was also on good terms with Oliver Cromwell's son Henry, who served as Lord Lieutenant.

After the Restoration, the same Oliver Fitzwilliam, who at that stage had succeeded his father as 2nd Viscount, served the Crown again and was created Earl of Tyrconnell by Charles II. It took some time, though, until he got his possessions back.

The Fitzwilliams had become Protestants shortly after the Reformation in Ireland, but this seems to have been a nominal change only as in 1600 they were regarded as Catholics again. They remained Catholic for around another hundred years. Finally, in 1710, Richard, 5th Viscount, conformed to the Established Church as he wanted to enter politics and take his seat in the House of Lords, which he could not do as a Catholic at that time.

His grandson, also Richard, who became the 7th Viscount Fitzwilliam, had an affair with a barmaid in his youth. His enraged father sent him on the Grand Tour and during his son's time on the Continent he arranged for the barmaid to marry somebody more suited to her social standing. When Richard came back he was devastated. He never married.

He followed his father as the developer of Merrion Road, Merrion Square and Fitzwilliam Square, where houses were built with bricks that were produced for decades in 'Lord Merrion's Brickfields'. One of those small brick manufactures was located where Sandymount Green is now.

The area had never been much above sea level. Digging clay for bricks lowered it even more. To protect it from frequent inundations, the 7th Viscount organised the construction of the sea wall from Merrion Gates northwards to the junction of Beach Road and Seapoint Avenue. He changed the name of the settlement from Brickfield Town to Sandymount and encouraged well-to-do Dublin citizens to build villas and residences there, so it could be said that he was the founder of Sandymount. The first residence that still exists in the area was built in 1789, two years before the sea wall. This house, which is now called Roslyn Park, was built for the landscape painter William Ashford. Ashford was a friend of the 7th Viscount, who let him have the land for a reasonable rent. Ashford was also a friend of the architect James Gandon, who provided plans for the residence.

The 7th Viscount Fitzwilliam was a connoisseur of paintings and amassed a big collection, which he willed to his alma mater, the University of Cambridge.

After his death, the title went in turn to his two younger brothers. Neither of the brothers had children. They would get the title, but Richard, 7th Viscount, obviously did not trust his brothers with the estate and so he had to look for another heir. His great-aunt had married Henry Herbert, 9th Earl of Pembroke, and her grandson George Augustus Herbert, 11th Earl of Pembroke, was Fitzwilliam's nearest blood relation. The English Earls of Fitzwilliam were very distant cousins. Richard Fitzwilliam invited both earls without telling them the reason for the proposed visit. He served them tea. The

Earl of Pembroke sipped his tea from the cup. The Earl of Fitzwilliam poured some of the tea from the cup into the saucer, blew on it to cool it and then slurped it from the saucer. The 7th Viscount Fitzwilliam is supposed to have muttered, 'Nobody who drinks tea like that will inherit my lands.' He died in 1816 and the Fitzwilliam Estate turned into the Pembroke Estate.

The cup which brought the Fitzwilliam lands to the Earls of Pembroke is still exhibited in Wilton House, the seat of the Earls of Pembroke in Wiltshire, England.

The end of the line of the Viscounts Fitzwilliam of Merrion is not always recorded exactly. Richard, 7th Viscount, had willed away his estate, but he could not will away his title. He was followed in the line of succession by his younger brother John, 8th Viscount, and John was succeeded by the next brother, Thomas, 9th Viscount. Upon the death, in 1833, of Thomas, 9th Viscount, the line of the Viscounts Fitzwilliam of Merrion and Barons Fitzwilliam of Thorncastle became extinct.

... AND THE HERBERTS

The Herbert family have held the title Earl of Pembroke (10th creation) since 1544. This family had a black sheep: in his youth, the 12th Earl secretly married a Sicilian princess. His father was enraged and had the marriage annulled. The erring son would inherit the title, but his younger half-brother would inherit the estate. The 12th Earl moved to Paris, never married again, but had at least seven illegitimate children by two different mistresses.

His half-brother Sidney Herbert was very important for the development of Sandymount. Herbert Road and Sydney Parade are named after him. Like the last Fitzwilliams the Herberts were regarded by some historians as 'crypto-Catholics'. They were High Church, as are the two churches that were built at the instigation of Sidney Herbert: St John the Evangelist in Sandymount and St Bartholomew in Ballsbridge. After Sidney Herbert's death, his widow converted to Roman Catholicism.

Many inhabitants of Sandymount who are interested in local history know that Sidney Herbert played a significant role in the development of the area. He is often referred to as the 'Earl of Pembroke', but he never held that title. He was a younger son of the 11th Earl of Pembroke, the half-brother of the 12th Earl and the father of the 13th, as well as the 14th Earl of Pembroke, but he never became an earl himself. At the end of his life, he was created Baron Herbert of Lea. Lea Road takes its name from this title.

Sidney Herbert relied very much on his agents for the Irish estates. In the beginning, this was Barbara Verschoyle, *née* Fagan, a Roman Catholic who was married to a Protestant. She had 'inherited' the position as agent from her parents, who had been agents for the Fitzwilliams. She herself had been the agent for Richard, 7th Viscount Fitzwilliam, and for George Herbert, 11th Earl of Pembroke, before becoming the agent for Sidney Herbert. Due to her influence, the Sisters of Charity were called to Sandymount to teach in a school for poor children that Barbara Verschoyle had founded. She also influenced Sidney Herbert in favour of Roman Catholics so that later he let the Roman Catholic Church have a site for what finally became Sandymount's parish church, Our Lady, Star of the Sea. The ground rent for this site was £10 per annum. The normal amount would have been around ten times as much.

Sidney Herbert was a friend of Florence Nightingale and as Secretary of State for War he reformed the life of soldiers in barracks under her influence. The first barracks to benefit from his reforms was Beggars' Bush Barracks, a short distance north-west of Sandymount.

PEMBROKE

When the area became a township in 1863, it took the name 'Pembroke Township' and the agent for the Pembroke Estate was an ex-officio commissioner of the township as the Earl of Pembroke was the landlord of 78 per cent of the area. Apart from the poorer north-east corner – that is, Ringsend and

Irishtown – the township housed many professionals, civil servants and merchants who wanted to live near the city but not in it. The conditions for the voting rights then ensured that the Township Commission was dominated by well-to-do Protestant Unionists. The members of the first commission had addresses in Dublin, Donnybrook, Merrion and Sandymount. One of them was the Sandymount developer Patrick Leahy, after whom Leahy's Terrace is named. The composition of the commission changed with the Local Government (Ireland) Act 1898, when the franchise was given to all male heads of households and lodgers and to female heads of households. This was not at all to the liking of the commissioners of Pembroke Township, whose chairman Fane Vernon, the agent of the Pembroke Estate, complained in 1892 to the Attorney General for Ireland that this law would give active and passive voting rights to all males of age, which might lead to what he called the 'spectacle' of a Board of Commissioners composed of 'inhabitants of cabins'.

Vernon's complaints were not listened to. Like many contemporaries in his class, he did not want the lower classes to have any political influence. On the other hand, the Pembroke Estates kept an eye on things in a very paternalistic way; for instance, by insisting in upholding certain quality standards in any housing development. If they were suspicious that this was not being done, they sent their own architects to check that their rules had been adhered to.

In 1911, one of the councillors of Pembroke Urban District Council was William F. Beckett, the father of the Nobel Prize winner Samuel Beckett. Another councillor was Loftus Lowcay Nuzum, JP, coal merchant, who, according to the 1901 census, then lived with his mother and younger brother in Prospect Terrace, Sandymount. The name might be familiar to people who frequently pass through Pearse Street as house no. 201, now used by Trinity College, still shows the inscription 'Nuzum Bros'.

The Pembroke Estate still exists, though most former tenants have by now bought out the ground rent.

Since the first cottages were built in around 1730, the village of Sandymount has grown continuously. Sandymount had around 220 houses in 1837, 520 in 1901, around 610 in 1911 and over 1,850 in 2012. Despite all the growth, Sandymount is still a green village.

MODERN ADMINISTRATION

Sandymount is an urban seaside village, but not an administrative unit. In the earliest days of the village, at the beginning of the eighteenth century, Brickfield/Sandymount was situated in the county of the City of Dublin. In 1840, Dublin Corporation was reformed and its area was reduced, with the canals as its borders. From then on, Sandymount was part of the Barony of Dublin in County Dublin. Baronies were divided into civil parishes. These were originally congruent with Church of Ireland parishes; later, both units could diverge. Sandymount was part of the parish of Donnybrook.

In 1863, it became part of Pembroke Township (from 1898, Pembroke Urban District) in the county of Dublin.

With the incorporation of Pembroke Urban District into Dublin Corporation in 1930, Sandymount became part of the City of Dublin and is now part of the postal district Dublin 4. Politically, Sandymount is governed by the South East Area Council (SEAC) of Dublin City Council (DCC). DCC is represented by the Lord Mayor of Dublin, but most of the administrative decisions are made by the non-elective Chief Executive of Dublin City Council. For local elections, Sandymount is part of the constituency of Pembroke-South Dock (eight councillors); in national elections, it was in the constituency of Dublin South-East (four TDs) until 2012 and since the reform of constituencies it has been in the constituency of Dublin Bay South (four TDs).

Both Roman Catholic parishes are in the Archdiocese of Dublin, with Sandymount's Star of the Sea in the deanery of Donnybrook and Merrion's Queen of Peace in the deanery of Dún Laoghaire as its main part was carved out of the parish of Booterstown. In the Church of Ireland Archdiocese of Dublin, Sandymount is part of the parish of Donnybrook and Irishtown, with the parish churches St Mary's in Donnybrook and St Matthew's in Irishtown and the trustee church St John the Evangelist in Sandymount.

The Presbyterian Congregation, which besides Sandymount includes Ringsend, Irishtown, Merrion, Ballsbridge and Donnybrook, belongs to the Dublin/Munster Presbytery. The Methodist Congregation, with an extension similar to the Presbyterian Congregation, belongs to the Dublin District. Presbyterians and Methodists have worshipped in Christ Church on Sandymount Green since the Presbyterian Church in Sandymount and the Methodist Church in Ringsend were demolished.

2

NATURE

Nature is everything around us that has not been made by men. It includes the universe, the sun and the earth, as well as microbes that cannot be seen without man-made instruments and sub-atomic particles, which cannot be seen at all.

The time spans over which nature works range from hundreds of millions of years, necessary to first form and then shape the limestone that lies under most of Ireland's surface, including Sandymount's, to a fraction of a second, the time it takes for lightning to strike.

GEOLOGY AND GEOGRAPHY

The shape of an area is described by geography, but the reason why it is as it is, its history over billions of years, is the subject of geology. Nearly every Irish person learns in primary school that Ireland is like a huge soup plate with a high (mountainous) rim and a deep wet inside. This description does not quite fit Sandymount, which is situated at the sea end of the Liffey plain. This is the area where the soup plate is flattened, as if a tin plate had been hit by a hammer. That way, the soup, or in this case the water, can get in and out. And so it does. More often than the inhabitants like.

As far as Sandymount is concerned, the water is not brought to the sea by the Liffey, but by the Dodder and some small streams. The Dodder's Irish name, 'An Dothra', might have something to do with the Irish word 'dothair', which means dark or evil. Indeed, it does often look dark and it has been evil at times, even along its lower and straightened course through Sandymount and on to the sea in Ringsend.

Geologically, the underlying bedrock is carboniferous limestone; not white, beige or pale grey, as is usual for limestone, but dark grey, perhaps because it includes carbonised plant particles. In Dublin, this type of rock is called 'calp' and many buildings have been built with it. The calp bedrock is covered by a thick layer of boulder clay. The clay was deposited by the sea and the boulders were rolled into it by the Ice Age. Before, during and after the Ice Age, the coastline changed many times. The eastern edge of the boulder clay in our area, roughly at Merrion Road, is an old coastline. Sandymount stretches out to the east from there. In other words, the Sandymount area has not been dry land for long at least not very long according to geological timelines. And if the sea level really will rise by 7m (23ft) because of global warming, Sandymount will have a big problem because the Sandymount DART station is only around 2.5m (8.2ft) above sea level and most of the village is even lower than that.

MARSH

The sea accumulated sand and silt with the result that land was eventually created where there had once been sea. This land stayed marshy and wet. Old maps show lots of little pools and even a biggish lake where St Alban's Park is now. The ground-water level still has to be monitored in this area and water has to be pumped away whenever it rises. An unobtrusive little pump house can be found between the railway and St Alban's Gardens, at the junction with St Alban's Park. The building bears a sign warning that it should not be interfered with. You know now why, so please don't!

The marshy land probably had alder and willow growing on it. The former, now gone, residence 'Mount Wil', as well as the extant 'Wilfield House', refer to the presence of willows. The original Lakelands is not much younger than Mount Wil and its name says a lot about the area.

People might wonder how pools could develop when the soil was so sandy, but there were also deposits of clay, which do not let the water through. Clay can be used in different ways, depending on its consistency and quality. The clay in this area was too coarse to be used for stoneware, but it was good for making bricks.

The village still had open fields in the twentieth century. Old inhabitants remember that the area where the Pet Hospital is now used to be the location of paddocks with horses and ponies in them.

'SANDYMOUNT'

The name 'Sandymount' was created by the landlords, the Viscounts Fitzwilliam. To entice well-to-do Dublin citizens to build residences and summer villas in the area (and pay a decent ground rent to the viscount as landlord), their perception of the area had to be diverted from clay and bricks.

Apart from clay, there is also a lot of sand in the area – so much so that when they built the Martello tower they could not find any bedrock under the sand, which caused a bit of a problem for the builders. So the 'sandy' part of the name is easy to understand. The 'mount' part is harder to explain. Perhaps the viscount wanted to keep the prospective tenants' minds off inundations (the newly built sea wall would help) and imply that the land was not really flat. There were similar names in the area. One of the old names was 'Scallet Hill'. The church of Our Lady, Star of the Sea, is supposed to be built on this 'hill', which probably rises not more than 3m (9.8ft) above the high waterline, but it seems to have been inundated less often than other places.

Apart from that, there is Dromard Avenue or Dromard Terrace, depending on which side of the street is considered. The word 'Dromard' contains the Irish words '*drom*', which means a ridge or the top, and '*árd*', which means a high, a hill or a top. Any 'ridge' or 'height' at this location cannot have been very high. The name probably refers to a small rise in the sand where the houses were built. The street leads down to the sea.

When the name 'Sandymount' was translated into Irish, the word chosen was '*dumhach*' (gen. '*duimhche*') which means a sandbank or a sand mound. Consequently, in old street name signs, Sandymount Avenue is '*Ascal na Duimhche*' in Irish. For some reason, the word '*dumhach*' does not seem to have been enough for officialdom. The official Irish name of the Sandymount DART stop is '*Dumhach Thrá*', with the word '*trá*' (strand) added to '*Dumhach*'. It is not known what the official name of Sandymount Strand is in Irish. In 2004, Dublin City Council published a book with the official names of streets in English and Irish. Sandymount Avenue, which used to be '*Ascal na Duimhche*' in Irish, is now '*Ascaill Dhumhach Thrá*'.

RABBITS

Soft sand heated by the sun but near water that keeps the lower layers of the sand moist enough to burrow into seems ideal for rabbits. And so it is, except that originally Ireland did not have rabbits. Hares are indigenous to Ireland; rabbits are not.

The rabbits came with the Normans, who loved them, both for their meat and their fur. Usually when people move, they want to take their creature comforts with them, which might explain why the Normans introduced rabbits to Ireland.

Foxes are indigenous to Ireland and foxes eat rabbits. The Normans knew this from England, as well as from Normandy. The solution was the rabbit warren. Suitable areas, sandy and near water, were fenced in and the rabbits were allowed to burrow there. Then, from time to time, ferrets were put into the warren to drive the rabbits into nets. You might say that the Normans farmed rabbits.

By the end of the seventeenth century, rabbit warrens declined, the fences disappeared and rabbits became feral. Now there are no more rabbits in Sandymount and it is highly likely that the foxes had something to do with that.

For a motorist who is not used to Sandymount, the place might still seem like a rabbit warren. Not many streets in the village are straight for any great length and there are many cul-de-sacs, some twisted, some interconnected.

FOXES AND SQUIRRELS

Foxes are indigenous in Ireland like hares. They are plentiful, with up to twenty individuals per square kilometre, even in suburban areas. Undisturbed green stretches along the railway seem to be where they have their dens. Before wheelie bins, when rubbish was put out on the road in plastic bags to be collected, foxes, as well as cats and stray dogs, would try to scratch open the bags and root around for anything edible. Some people feared that foxes would disappear with the introduction of wheelie bins. This did not happen. It is not for nothing that in nearly all European fables and folk tales the fox is regarded as the most cunning animal. Foxes found ways to survive and Sandymount should be grateful to foxes as they help to keep the rodent population down.

Occasionally foxes can be seen in daylight, patrolling gardens and meandering along garden walls the same way cats do. At dusk or dawn they even trot down the streets and they have even been seen crossing the busy Merrion Road without much concern for the traffic.

Squirrels do the same thing, hopping across roads and up onto garden walls, but usually they are faster and more nervous than foxes. No wonder, for foxes hunt squirrels and cats have been known to do the same. Luckily for the squirrel, it can climb faster than a cat and it can jump from branch to branch with more ease.

Squirrels are indigenous to Ireland, but only the red or European squirrels. They are supposed to have lived in Ireland since before the last ice age. They became nearly extinct in the seventeenth century and were reintroduced in the nineteenth century. Since 1911, the grey or American squirrel has been gaining on the red squirrel. Grey squirrels are bigger and less shy than red squirrels and they seem to push the red squirrels out of the habitats they invade. In Sandymount, only grey squirrels remain.

DOGS

The only wild animal of the dog family is the fox. All other dogs are domesticated, which is especially true of Sandymount, where dogs are well behaved even when not on a lead. Their owners clean up after them in general. The strand is the main area where dogs can run uninhibited. Legally they should not be let off the lead as the whole strand is a bird protection area, but where else in the area can dogs run free?

CATS

There are also many cats in Sandymount. They all have a home but during the day they roam outside and are seen patrolling garden walls. Like foxes, they are good at keeping the rodent population down. Despite the presence of foxes, cats and garden walls, sometimes mice manage to get into gardens and/ or houses. During harsh winters, they even can be seen running up tree trunks and along branches to get at the bird feeders.

BIRDS

There are many birds in Sandymount: sea birds and waders on the strand as well as garden birds. Dublin Bay is a famous wintering place for arctic sea birds, especially Brent Geese. Nearly all the population of brent geese from the High Arctic of Canada spend their winters in Ireland and a good number of them come to Dublin Bay. They can usually be seen between October and April. It is always a spectacle when one sees flocks of more than 100 geese flying across the Dublin skies, honking loudly, sometimes following the course of the Liffey to meadows further inland when they have finished with their favourite food, the eel grass in Dublin Bay.

The sea in the Sandymount area supports at least three different types of gulls: laughing gulls, herring gulls and greater black-backed gulls. Terns and oystercatchers can be found all year round. In winter curlews, godwits, turnstones, sanderlings and dunlins appear as well.

Seabirds and waders have got used to the dogs on the strand. Much more dangerous, especially for nesting birds and bird eggs, are the foxes that roam the dunes near Merrion Gates. Rats that live between the boulders that secure the Promenade and the sea wall eat bird eggs and young birds as well.

It is a special sight to watch a heron flying overhead, with its slow and rhythmic wing beat, its long S-shaped neck and its legs trailing behind its body. It is even funnier to see a heron walking along the roof ridge on top of a house.

As far as garden birds are concerned, their number increases considerably when birds from further north come to winter here. Redwings from Iceland and Scandinavia are common in Sandymount in the winter; waxwings from Finland and Siberia can sometimes be observed in the same gardens, but only in very cold weather.

Heron on a rooftop.

Raptors are rare, though sparrowhawks appear and have occasionally been observed taking blackbirds in people's back gardens.

PLANTS

Sandymount is a green village
with plenty of trees, bushes and
other plants. Most of the greenery
is private, but there are trees on public
land like holm oak and big hebe bushes
along the Promenade.   *Holm oak.*

The green look of the streets is caused by
private front gardens, some of which have magnificent
trees shadowing the road, including eucalyptus trees and
tall black pines. Some of the older streets are planted with
London plane (for instance, Sandymount Road) and there are
sycamore trees on a stretch of Sydney Parade. Some of these
have grown very tall and their roots occasionally damage the
pavement. In the twenty-first century, Dublin City Council
planted some more trees along streets in the newer parts of
Sandymount. According to the original plan, each of the
streets that were included in the plan was to get a different
variety of tree. In the end, the trees chosen were all of the
same type: Corylus colurna or Turkish hazel, which has lately
become quite common as a street tree. Those trees have a
symmetrical, pyramidal shape, a structured bark and, like
any other trees and bushes of the hazel family, pollen that is
highly allergenic.

Many of the trees and bushes planted in Sandymount
gardens are not indigenous and have sometimes been
introduced from faraway places, like the Cordyline from New
Zealand. Cordylines seed themselves vigorously and it is best
to remove unwanted seedlings as quickly as possible as the
roots grow deep in a very short time.

To find indigenous and wild plants, one should not only
search on the ground. Some ferns and other plants manage
to grow in the cracks of garden walls and on top of the walls.

Plants that grow where they are not wanted, e.g. in flower beds and lawns, lanes or even in the cracks of the footpaths, are called weeds. None of them are useless. The unloved stinging nettles, for instance, provide food for caterpillars and brave people can use the young top leaves for soup or even as a vegetable. Dandelion leaves can be eaten as salad, though it should be remembered that dandelion is a diuretic.

Lesser sea-spurrey.

Sometimes plants are overlooked because they are small. Many have beautifully coloured flowers, like the low-growing scarlet pimpernel and blue pimpernel, both of the primrose family. Equally small is the sea-spurrey, with its pink flowers, sometimes found at the sea edge of the Promenade.

Sea aster, red valerian and rock samphire can be found on the strand, as well as marram grass. The Promenade has sycamores growing on its seaside border. Dublin City Council lets them grow as their roots secure the big boulders. The City Council is very careful, though, to cut those sycamores rigorously so that they remain low-growing bushes.

Lanes and some grassy spots show white daisies and yellow buttercups, as well as hawkweeds, sow thistles and groundsel. Plants with small or with green flowers, like those of the sorrel or the plantain family, are usually completely overlooked.

RIVER AND SEA

The fishing rights in the Dodder are reserved and there are no reports of humans fishing on its shore in the Sandymount area, even though the river contains trout and grey mullet. The fishing is left to the gulls, the herons and the occasional kingfisher. There also are grey wagtails, mallards and moorhens and sometimes a redshank, as well as various gulls.

Aquatic life is less easy to observe. Sometimes little crabs can be seen scuttling around in shallow water and the weird-looking heaps of sand piled up by ragworms and lugworms are ubiquitous. Both of those worms are dug up for bait. Shells of different types, including whelks, prove that a lot of shellfish live further out.

Today no fishing is done on the strand anymore. In earlier times, Sandymount Strand was known for its herring, its shrimp and its cockles. The fishing rights were held by the landlords, the Fitzwilliams, who, when they leased the fishing rights out to somebody else, included '500 choice herrings per year' in the rent due to them. They obviously knew what they were doing as in the first half of the nineteenth century D'Alton reported that the herrings from Dublin Bay were sweeter and oilier than herrings from either Wales or Scotland. At least since the 1970s, the amount of herrings in the Irish Sea has decreased considerably.

Shrimp are no longer present in this area, but this has nothing to do with overfishing. In the severe winter of 1741, known as 'the hard frost', shrimp disappeared completely and never returned.

Cockles are abundant and were still collected and eaten until some decades ago. This is no longer advisable, at least until the pollution of Dublin Bay has decreased. It has been discovered that shellfish can survive even after accumulating an amount of pollutants that would be lethal for humans. One study suggested that this type of enteric poisoning could have been the cause of the fever that killed Molly Malone.

There must still be a good number of fish in Dublin Bay as there are quite a few seals around. Sandymount Strand is too flat for them to come near, but occasionally, when the tide is high, a dark head can be spotted further out.

THE BULL

Sandymount Strand is one of the greatest amenities Sandymount has to offer. For the extended village, the strand is

2km (1.2 miles) long (1km (0.6 miles) for the core village) and up to 2km wide, at least at low tide. At high tide it disappears nearly completely.

The vast expanses of sand at low tide in Dublin Bay were given the name 'The Bull' as the sound of the incoming tide, especially with a strong east wind blowing, was supposed to be like the roaring of a bull.

The expanse of sand is cut into a northern and a southern part by the River Liffey. After the building of the North Bull Wall, part of the North Bull turned into North Bull Island. The South Bull stayed tidal even after the completion of the South Bull Wall. Cut through by Cock Lake, it extends up to 2km (1.2 miles) eastwards from the sea wall at low tide, but is completely covered by water at high tide. Because of sandbanks and tidal inlets, it can be dangerous for people to walk out too far at low tide.

Most of the sand of the Bull is firm enough to walk on. Near the Merrion Gates, some silt is mixed in with the sand, which makes it a bit slippery, especially as it stays wet longer than sand would normally, but it is still firm enough to walk on. The silt at the northern end of the strand is a different case. At low tide, it looks as if you might be able to walk across from Sandymount to the eastern end of Irishtown Nature Park or even to the South Wall. It is not advisable to do so. This stretch has patches with lots of silt and hardly any sand. Those patches don't dry out properly and are not firm enough even for big dogs. Any walker will sink deeper and deeper with each step. So, dear reader, do not try it.

COCK LAKE

Cock Lake, also called Cockle Lake and sometimes even Cork Lake, has been known by this name since at least the seventeenth century. It is not a lake at all. On old maps, different courses of Cock Lake are shown. On maps printed before the building of the South Wall, Cock Lake is an arm of the Liffey, starting at Ringsend, running eastwards to where the Pigeon House is now and then turning south to reach the sea at low water at Merrion Gates. On the 1760 map of John Rocque, it is shown as a loop in the South Bull shaped like the letter 'C' with the northern mouth near the Piles (the predecessors of the South Wall) and the southern mouth opposite Merrion Gates. This course would have made half the South Bull an island at low tide. Later maps, such as the John Taylor's 1816 map, show the original course of a Liffey arm, even though Cock Lake is cut off from the Liffey by the South Wall. Despite that, Taylor shows it starting at Ringsend and running parallel to the South Wall as far as the Pigeon House, where it swings in a semicircle first south and then east to reach the sea at low water opposite where the lake at St Alban's Park once was. On other nineteenth-century maps, Cock Lake is not as curved as on Taylor's map, but goes more or less in a straight line southwards from the Pigeon House to the low water mark opposite Merrion Gates. John Rocque shows that the pool where St Alban's Park is now was connected to Cock Lake. One train of thought is that when this pool's connection with Cock Lake was cut off, the course of Cock Lake was altered. Today, after the latest land reclamation, the northernmost part no longer exists and the course is straight southwards from the eastern end of Irishtown Nature Park, near the Pigeon House, and reaches the sea opposite Merrion Gates. Cock Lake does not dry out, even at the lowest tide. In places, it can be quite deep and causes dangerous situations when the tide comes in as people do not always realise how deep the lake has become in time.

TIDES AND SANDBANKS

In former times, Dublin Bay was famous, or rather infamous, for its sandbanks, many of which shifted frequently. Most of the problems they caused for ships have been eliminated by the North and South Bull walls, as well as by lighthouses.

The sandbanks are still dangerous, even if not for ships. They cause danger to people who do not know Sandymount Strand well. The vast expanse of sand of the South Bull at low tide makes it very tempting to walk far out to the water's edge.

The danger is that some people do not realise that these vast expanses of sand are slightly undulated and include sandbanks which rise over the rest of the sand. These sandbanks can turn into temporary islands when the tide comes in and disappear completely when the water rises higher. During the last few years there have been some incidents that were not only reported locally but made the national newspapers and radio stations. People suddenly found themselves on a sandbank completely surrounded by water and had to be rescued by the Dún Laoghaire lifeboat or by helicopter. In one case, a friendly garda carried a terrified child across the water, which, at its deepest point, reached up to the garda's hips. The parents of the child were taken aboard the lifeboat shortly after their child had been safely carried to the strand.

Until access to the strand at Merrion Gates was closed for motorcars, one car per year, on average, was lost on the strand when the surrounding water had risen too high to drive the car back.

Sandymount Strand has a sign warning that it might be dangerous to walk more than 200m (650ft) further out from that sign. At high tide, this sign is completely surrounded by water, which often causes consternation among people who are visiting Sandymount Strand for the first time.

The average tidal range in Dublin Bay is 3.5m (11ft). On Sandymount Strand, the water reaches the sea wall or the Promenade at high tide; at low tide, it can be up to 2km (1.2 miles) away. People who do not live beside the sea do not realise how quickly the tide rises and how fast the waterline moves inland.

During the six hours of rising tide, the waterline will approach the land at an average speed of 167m (548ft) per hour or 2.75m (9ft) per minute. Vertically, the water rises nearly 0.6m (2ft) per hour or 10mm (0.4in) per minute. Somebody who has walked out on the strand to a higher sandbank may have paddled through water that was 300mm (12in) deep at low tide, reaching halfway up his or her calf. Returning an hour later, he or she will have to pass through the same spot, which could be 600mm (24in) deep at that point, reaching halfway up his or her thigh (and an hour later it would reach his or her hip).

PUBLIC STRAND

Sandymount Strand is the biggest public area in Sandymount and also the oldest and the only one that is not man-made. It is triangular in shape with the north side parallel to Seán Moore Park and Irishtown Nature Park. From there, the other two sides of the triangle go south and south-west until they meet at Merrion Gates. Some parts of the South Bull belong in the north to Ringsend and Irishtown and in the south to Booterstown, all with their own strands.

At low tide, Sandymount Strand has an area of nearly $2km^2$. At high tide, however, the only corner that is not covered by water is a small stretch near the Solar Pillar dedicated to James Joyce. The strand is a great amenity, not only for the people of Sandymount. Many come from other areas, especially in the summer when they can walk on the sandbanks or paddle through Cock Lake. At times riders can be seen galloping along the strand and people go there to practise their hurling or even their golf strokes. Quad bikes or ponies and traps sometimes appear, especially when the strand is not crowded.

In the winter, walkers stay nearer the land edge of the strand and leave the rest to thousands, if not millions, of birds.

A mishap while kite surfing on Sandymount Strand.

PROMENADE/DVS

The Promenade at Sandymount Strand came into existence because of the Dodder Valley Sewer (DVS) which was completed in 1973. Dublin County Council had decided to take the sewage from Tallaght and places even further up the Dodder in pipes down to Merrion Strand. The main sewer from the Dodder Valley leaves the Dodder at Clonskeagh and is led underground, through Donnybrook, Ballsbridge and Sandymount, until it reaches the coast at Merrion. There it follows the sea wall unto the point where Gilford Avenue meets Strand Road. From this point, pipes laid in the sand under the sea take the sewage to the sewage plant in Ringsend.

Unsurprisingly, Sandymount and Merrion residents raised objections to any disfiguration of their strand. To overcome this opposition, the pipes were covered by a long, narrow strip of reclaimed land. A promenade, around 1km (½ mile) long and 25m (80ft) wide, was built from where the pipes reach the strand in Merrion to the point where the pipes leave the strand to go across the sands of the South Bull to the waste water facilities on Poolbeg Peninsula.

This promenade is officially free of bikers, roller skaters and skateboarders so one can walk up and down and rest or play on the grass strip between the strand and the sea wall. Manhole covers still show the letters 'DVS'.

For many years, the Promenade has been part of the east coast '*Slí na Sláinte*', an Irish Heart Foundation initiative, and in 2014 outdoor gym equipment was erected.

MARTELLO TOWER

What are Martello towers for? When asked that question, a sailor on board a nineteenth-century packet boat replied, 'The devil a use I can think of, but to please Mr. Windham [Secretary of War] and puzzle posterity'.

Sandymount Martello tower is officially situated on Merrion townland, but it has been known as Sandymount

Tower at least since the time when it was the terminus of the nos 3 and 4 tramlines. It is bigger than most other Martello towers as it is one of the few that were built for two cannons. The measurements are 15m (50ft) in external diameter with a wall thickness of 3m (10ft). This results in an internal space of 9m (30ft) in diameter. Originally the tower had no openings at all on the ground floor. It was entered on the land side at first-floor level through a door that was later reached by an external winding metal stairway 0.9m (3ft) wide. Machicolations above the door gave those in the garrison the possibility of dropping stones and hot oil onto the heads of attackers who attempted to enter by force.

The living quarters for the garrison of twelve men were on the first floor. The ground floor was reached by a stairway 1.2m (4ft) in diameter within the wall. The ground floor held the kitchen and the master gunner's stores, as well as the magazine, where thirty barrels of gunpowder could be held. Beneath this floor was a water storage tank. The vaulted stone roof was protected by a parapet and reached via helical stairs. The roof held two 24-pounder guns, mounted on a roller system so they could be aimed in any direction over Dublin Bay. There also was a shot furnace that could make cannonballs red-hot in order to set the sails and timber of ships on fire.

Modern excavations show that the walls were founded on a massive network of pitch-pine beams, arranged in three layers, rather than bedrock.

A small annex to the tower on the bay side contained an external privy, an ash pit and a coal store. There was also an internal privy built into the thickness of the circular wall.

Cooking was done on an open fire. It is not known whether the thirty barrels of gunpowder in the room next to the kitchen made the cook nervous.

In 1806, the tower's cannons were tested and in the same year the garrison engaged in a military exercise that included the Pigeon House Fort and some horse artillery. During this exercise, both cannons fired across Sandymount Strand. This was probably the only time the canons were used. They never saw action against an enemy. Sandymount and Williamstown towers were disarmed in 1865.

The first owner of the tower had been the War Department, which had bought the ground from the Fitzwilliam Estate and marked its property with border stones, one of which survives. After its decommission in the 1860s, the tower was rented to the Earl of Pembroke, who used it as a residence for some of his staff. Some of the Earl of Pembroke's staff still lived there in the beginning of the twentieth century and the *Irish Independent* reported on 16 December 1906:

> Peter McKenna, a motorman from the Tramway Company, heard cries for assistance issuing from the building. On investigation he found Denis Molloy, the aged caretaker, and his wife Mary imprisoned inside. They had mislaid the key on Saturday morning and were unable to regain excess. … Then the Earl of Pembroke's steward, … accompanied by seven of his men, went to the tower, but although the latter used crowbars, they failed to open the big door owing to its great strength, and the manner in which it was bolted. Finally they got on the roof with the aid of a ladder, and got into the room in which Molloy and his wife were by means of a spiral staircase. They were able to force the lock of the door downstairs, and release the couple.

The original door on the first floor is now a window. The Dublin Tramways Company bought the tower and broke through the walls to create ground-floor doors in the twentieth century, even though the steel door facing south is inscribed with the year 1822.

At some time, the tower was used as a café and a shop. A new annex was built in the 1990s, possibly with the view of opening a café or a restaurant again, but that did not happen. Nowadays the tower is not in use and remains locked.

Tourists are sometimes disappointed that they cannot gain entrance, usually because they have mixed it up with Sandycove Tower, which was made famous by James Joyce's *Ulysses*.

TWIN BARBER POLES

The two chimneys of the Poolbeg power station, called 'The Twin Barber Poles' because of their red and white hoops, are no longer in use and for years there was talk of demolishing them. Many people were not happy about the idea and after a lengthy campaign the chimneys were given protected status. They are not identical twins. One was built in 1969 and the other in 1977. They are both of nearly equal height, 207.48m (680.7ft) and 207.8m (681.7ft). The older one has a diameter of 13.8m (45.3ft) at the base and 4.8m (15.7ft) at the top, while the diameter of the younger one is 15.6m (51.2ft) at the base and 6.7m (21.9ft) at the top. They both stopped working in 2010 and have been protected structures since July 2014.

Though they stand in Ringsend, they are part of the Sandymount scenery as they can be seen from everywhere on Sandymount Strand and can also often be seen from the streets of Sandymount.

Some people are indifferent to them, but for many they are a powerful symbol. 'When I see them from the plane, I know I am home.'

Twin Barber Poles, Sandymount Strand.

3

EDUCATION AND WORK

EDUCATION

In the nineteenth century, well-to-do inhabitants of Sandymount employed tutors for their children before they sent their boys to boarding schools and university and their girls to 'finishing schools', in Switzerland if possible. Poor families had no money for education. Still, even in the first half of the nineteenth century, schools are mentioned in descriptions in texts such as Samuel Lewis's *Topographical Dictionary* or even on maps like in the first Ordnance Survey map of 1837, which has 'School Ho.' beside the building that later became the courthouse, then the post office and is now an estate agent's office.

FORMER SCHOOLS

It is unknown what type of school the 'School Ho.' mentioned on the first Ordnance Survey map of 1837 was. Samuel Lewis writes about three schools in Sandymount:

> In the village there are a parochial school, erected in 1833, and supported by subscription, and a female school, built and supported by the Misses Hepenstall, aided by £100 from the Lord Lieutenant's fund. A branch of the Sisters of Charity, from Stanhope-street, Dublin, established themselves in Sandymount Avenue about five years since; the inmates

consist of a superioress and five nuns, who instruct about
80 children: a neat chapel attached is open to the public.

The parochial school was a school of the Church of Ireland
parish, in this case St Mary's of Donnybrook. The Sisters of
Charity are an order of Catholic nuns and the superioress Lewis
mentions was the founder of the order, Mother Mary Aikenhead.
The 1837 Ordnance Survey map shows a 'New Grove Seminary'
at the place where Newgrove Avenue meets Strand Road.

In his talk 'From Scallet Hill to Brickfield Town', read to
the Old Dublin Society in January 1985, Kevin P. O'Rorke
mentioned that in the last half of the nineteenth century
Sandymount had become 'a regular haven for private
schools', of which he recorded the Sandymount Academical
Institution (a Presbyterian College in the castle); Miss Abbot's
Ladies Academy, 20 Sandymount Green; Miss Whammond's
Ladies Seminary on Claremont Road; Sandymount College
School, also on Claremont Road; Sandymount Classical and
Mathematical Academy on Newgrove Avenue; Miss Clarke's
Ladies Seminary on Sandymount Road; and a boarding school
for young men at Prospect House on Prospect Terrace.

The same list of schools appears in exactly the same words
and with the same addresses in an earlier brochure by Saunders
and Bradshaw, entitled 'Sandymount' and dated March 1975.
What both texts call the Sandymount Academical Institution
was listed in Thom's Official Directory for 1889 under 'Greer,
William, Sandymount Academical Institute, Sandymount'.
According to the 1901 census, William A. Greer, widower,
ran a school for boys with him as headmaster, five teachers
and his sister Annie Greer as housekeeper. The school then
had twenty-five boarding pupils aged 10 to 16 years. Despite
the fact that Saunders and Bradshaw and later O'Rorke
called it 'a Presbyterian College', only ten of the pupils were
Presbyterian; the other fifteen were described as 'Protestant
Episcopalian'. Of the five teachers, three were Presbyterian
and two Episcopalian. In the 1911 census, William Greer is not
mentioned; the school is run by Annie Greer as principal, with
three teachers. Two boarders are mentioned, but the school is
described as 'Pembroke Day School'.

20 Sandymount Green.

O'Rorke gives '20, Sandymount Green' as the address of Miss Abbot's Ladies Academy. This is the address of the building described as 'School Ho.' in the 1837 Ordnance Survey map.

The 1901 census mentions a 'school' on Claremont Road and a 'Methodist School' on Newgrove Avenue. The census also mentions a 'Private School' on Sandymount Road in a building that has Miss Charlotte Clarke, teacher, as resident; this is probably O'Rorke's 'Miss Clarke's Ladies Seminary'. Also mentioned in the 1901 census is an 'Academical School' on Star of the Sea Terrace, which was the name of a part of Sandymount Road. This might have been O'Rorke's 'Sandymount Classical and Mathematical Academy'. None of those schools exist today.

Sandymount High School
Sandymount High School is no longer in existence either, even though it was established much later than the aforementioned schools. It was a non-denominational, co-educational secondary school on Herbert Road, founded in 1947 on the site the 1907 Ordnance Survey map shows as the residence 'Riverside', which, according to the 1901 and 1911 censuses, was the home of James Beckett, head of the well-known family of builders.

Sandymount High School was privately owned by the Cannon family. Patrick Cannon was the first principal. He was succeeded in that position by his son Conall. Sandymount

High School was chosen by parents who did not want to send their children to denominational and/or same-sex schools. It also had foreign nationals as pupils, which was a rarity in the vast majority of Irish schools until the late 1990s.

The then Catholic Archbishop of Dublin, John Charles McQuaid, was opposed to non-denominational and also to co-educational schools and organised the foundation of Marian College next door to Sandymount High School as a direct competitor for (male) students.

Sandymount High School suffered and had to close in 1999. The land where the school had been was sold and an apartment block built on the site was named Cannon Place to commemorate the family that had owned the school. The Olympic gold medal-winner Ronnie Delany had been a pupil of Sandymount High School.

Roslyn Park
From 1950, the building that had originally been called Sandymount Park housed a secondary school for girls, which was run by the Sisters of the Sacred Heart of Mary. They named the house Roslyn Park. As the old building did not have sufficient space for the school, more buildings were erected in the neighbourhood of the old house. To allow for this, another old house on the grounds had to be demolished. This school closed in 1982.

EXISTING SCHOOLS

Montessori Schools
Gilford Montessori School was founded in 1991 by a trained Montessori teacher in her home. In 2008, her niece joined her and they founded the Montessori School and After School. For over a year, they used rooms in the Railway Union Sports Club, but in late summer 2009 they moved into purpose-built facilities in Lakelands.

Strand Montessori School has existed since 2011, when it was founded by two trained Montessori teachers. They provide Montessori education, after-school care and holiday camps. Their rooms are in Merrion Hall, near the strand and Merrion Gates.

Primary Schools

St Matthew's
St Matthew's National School is the oldest primary school that still exists in (the extended area of) Sandymount. The school's first schoolhouse was built in 1832 on Irishtown Road beside Dodder Terrace in the village of Irishtown. The school was for boys only. In 1904, a schoolhouse for girls was opened on the other side of Dodder Terrace, opposite the boys' school. In 1951, the boys' and girls' schools merged and in 1959 they moved into a new complex between Cranfield Place and Church Avenue. This complex was enlarged a couple of times in subsequent years, notably in 1969, when the school merged with St Stephen's School on Northumberland Road. St Matthew's National School now has eight classes.

Scoil Mhuire
Scoil Mhuire, the Sandymount National School for girls, has a history almost as long as that of St Matthew's National School. It began in the early 1830s on Sandymount Lane as a school for the poor children in the neighbourhood. It was run by the Sisters of Charity, on the instigation of Mrs Barbara Verschoyle, the agent for the landlord Sidney Herbert. When the Sisters of Charity moved to Lakelands in 1876, the school moved with them and merged with the school that the Carmelite Sisters had run there since 1856. At that stage, the school was called St Mary's National School for Girls. At the beginning of the twentieth century, it was accessed from Park Avenue (no. 26a, according to the 1911 census). In 1972, the school was in need of upgrading, but as a result of the report of the architect, the Department of Education decided to build a new school, which was opened in the grounds of Lakelands in 1974. From then on, it has been called Scoil Mhuire. Its address is now Gilford Road. Since 1993, the principal has been a lay person and in 1998 the school was handed over to

the parish. Scoil Mhuire is very good at GAA sports and the girls have won a number of tournaments.

Star of the Sea

The youngest of the national schools in Sandymount is the Star of the Sea School for boys. The ground where it stands was acquired in 1850, but the school was only built in 1878. Originally the Christian Brothers were supposed to run the school, but they declined the offer and the Board of Education took over. The school was enlarged in 1891 and again in 1905, when it was renamed Canon O'Hanlon Memorial School in honour of Canon John O'Hanlon, who had been the parish priest for twenty-five years until his death in May 1905. The rooms built in 1905 now form the school hall.

In 1974 a new school was built, the junior and senior schools were amalgamated and the school was renamed St Mary's, Star of the Sea BNS. The Star of the Sea School has good contacts with the local GAA club and, like Scoil Mhuire, has won many Gaelic sports prizes.

Secondary Schools

Marian College

Since the closure of the school of the Sisters of the Sacred Heart of Mary in Roslyn Park and Sandymount High School, the only secondary school left in Sandymount is Marian College. Marian College was founded in the early 1950s, when John Charles McQuaid, Catholic Archbishop of Dublin, invited the Marist Brothers to open a school in the Sandymount/Ballsbridge area as a Catholic alternative to the private co-educational and non-denominational Sandymount High School, as neither non-denominational nor co-educational schools were in favour with the Roman Catholic hierarchy. The school was built on grounds bordering the railway, the Dodder, Herbert Road and the competing Sandymount High School.

Marian College was opened in 1954, with one class per year. It grew steadily over the years and since 1970 it has had three classes per year. The school is well known for its sports teams, especially its water polo team, which practises in the school's own swimming pool. This pool is open to the public at certain times and for some years was used by the Irish national rugby team, who practised in the old Lansdowne Road Stadium next door (though across the Dodder).

Brothers Niall and Kevin O'Brien of Railway Union Cricket and members of the Irish national cricket team were pupils of Marian College and so was Diarmuid Martin, Archbishop of Dublin.

School for Special Needs

The Enable Ireland School in Sandymount has a history that reaches back for decades. Still known locally as 'The Clinic', the Enable Ireland Sandymount School provides services for children with a primary physical disability and/or developmental delay. The expression 'Clinic' stems from earlier times. Cerebral Palsy Ireland (CPI) was established in 1948 by Dr William Robert Fitzgerald Collis. In 1952, he founded a school in Sandymount for sufferers of cerebral palsy. This school had Christie Brown, the author of the book *My Left Foot*, as a pupil occasionally. In the year the school was founded, the name 'CPI' was changed to 'National Association for Cerebral Palsy'. In 1953, this association moved to St Brendan's School-Clinic in Sandymount. On maps of the nineteenth century, this site shows a building with the name 'The Cottage'.

A couple of years after the move, the buildings of St Brendan's School-Clinic became inadequate for the new purpose. In the 1960s, a new school was built, which soon again was regarded as unsuitable according to new ideas about cerebral palsy. The building that exists today was opened in 1999 by the then Minister for Health and Children, Brian Cowen, TD.

Enable Ireland School Sandymount is a Department of Education special school under the patronage of Enable Ireland. The school has a long tradition and considerable expertise in the care and education of children with complex needs and offers specialised teaching and individual programmes. It also has an integrated preschool called 'Little Pals', which offers preschool services to children with a primary physical disability who attend Enable Ireland, Sandymount, and also accepts local children without a disability between the ages of 2 to 5 years, with twelve places in each group, six for Enable Ireland children and six for local children.

WORK

Sandymount is a residential suburban seaside village. Any work done there, apart from the rather regular digging-up of one road or another is done unobtrusively inside a house, shop or workshop. In earlier times, however, there were some bigger work sites.

Bricks

Brickmaking pre-dates Sandymount. Bricks were made in this area roughly between 1735 and 1785 in what was called 'Lord Merrion's Brick Fields' on old maps.

Brickmaking was seasonal on smaller brickfields, with a production period from April to September. The clay was dug out of the clay pit and left for a few days to sour. In smaller brickfields like the pits in Lord Merrion's Brickfields, the clay was then worked to the right consistency by watering and trampling it, which was called tempering. The clay was then put into wooden moulds, which were shod in iron and left to harden. When they were sufficiently hardened, the bricks were arranged in hacks to dry, long rows consisting of small stacks five bricks high and one brick wide. Next the bricks were stacked so that a fire could be lit under them, called a clamp. That was and is the traditional way to fire bricks.

Around what is now Sandymount Green, a small settlement of brick workers and their families grew. This settlement was called 'Brickfield' or 'Brickfield Town'. According to a 1766 survey, ten families lived there, half of them described as 'Protestants', the other half as 'Papists'.

When the clay ran out at the end of the eighteenth century, Viscount Fitzwilliam decided to develop the area as a residential area for well-to-do people and re-named it 'Sandymount'.

The digging of clay had lowered the level of the ground and increased the danger of inundation by the sea. To protect against such flooding, the 7th Viscount Fitzwilliam of Merrion had the sea wall built in 1791.

Distilling

Lots of small distilleries existed in and around Dublin in the eighteenth century. One of them was the Dodderbank Distillery on the right bank of the Dodder, where Sandymount Hotel is now. This was bought in 1795 by Robert Haig (1764–1845). Haig was a member of one of the three big Scottish distiller families, Haig, Jameson and Stein, which were all interconnected. Robert Haig's mother was Margaret Stein and Robert's sister Margaret married John Jameson. Robert Haig became the uncle of John Haig, the founder of the well-known Scottish distillery, and the brother-in-law of John Jameson of the Bow Street Distillery in Dublin.

At the end of the eighteenth century, some of those Scottish distillers moved to Ireland, including Robert Haig, who bought the Dodderbank Distillery in 1795. Haig enlarged it so that it became one of the big distilleries in the Dublin area, of the same class and size as the distilleries of the Jamesons, the Powers and the Roes.

In the early 1820s, the output was low, but after 1823 it increased enormously, at least for a time. Mother Mary Aikenhead wrote on 30 December 1833 that this distillery had employed eight families, but that those families now had to pawn their clothes and furniture as the distillery had closed. Another source states, however, that in 1833 Robert Haig had added an early Coffey still to his pot stills and that in this year he raised his output to 1.5 million litres (330,000 gallons) per annum. He constantly had problems with revenue, which, along with the temperance movement, led to the closing of the distillery in the 1840s.

Robert Haig is buried on the old Donnybrook graveyard. The headstone of his grave describes him as sixth in descent from James Haig of Bemersyde, Berwickshire. The gravestone also informs us that Robert Haig and his wife Caroline Mary, *née* Wolseley, had thirteen children, three of whom died in infancy. The other seven sons and three daughters grew up, married and most of them survived their father Robert.

Other Industries

In the first years of the Dublin & Kingstown Railway, this company had building and repairing works for engines and wagons where the Railway Cottages are now. Those works later moved to the vicinity of Grand Canal Dock.

Thereafter, Sandymount as a residential village did not, and to this day does not, have an industrial area. The *Official Industrial Directory of the Department of Industry and Commerce* of 1955 mentions some smaller concerns in Sandymount:

Francis J. McNally: 10 Newgrove Avenue, Sandymount (leather dog collars, leads, muzzles, etc.)

The National Vaccination Institute: 80 Sandymount Road (medical and pharmaceutical preparations as well as vaccination packs)

Richardson, Tee, Rycroft & Co. (Dublin) Ltd: 17 Gilford Road, Sandymount (producers of knitted cotton fabric and of underwear)

Storys (Ireland) Ltd: Willow Lodge, Park Avenue (thermal storage heaters)

These firms are no longer found in Sandymount and some of them do not exist anymore.

Today, Beach Ironworks on Beach Road produces steel doors and grids, railings and different types of gates, including automated electric gates and fire escapes. Ailesbury Auto Services is a small garage on Beach Road that does all sorts of car repairs. Also in the automobile line is an official Renault dealer on Beach Road, on the corner of Church Avenue in the extended Sandymount area. Seafort Avenue, right in the village centre, has a very good craft picture-framing shop.

Nurseries

The 1837 Ordnance Survey map shows a nursery in the extended village, between Serpentine Avenue in the north, the railway in the east, Sandymount Lane in the south and Merrion Road in the west. In the 1907 map this area was built up and residential.

The 1901 census lists a family named Jameson in Park Avenue. The 46-year-old father is described as a nurseryman and florist and his 23-year-old daughter as a florist. In 1911, the family was still at no. 19 Park Avenue. The 56-year-old father is still a nurseryman, his two daughters, 33 and 24 years old, are florists and a 20-year-old son is a nurseryman. The same building houses an older son, aged 23, with his own family in a separate household. This son is listed as a nurseryman too.

The 1907 map shows 'Royal Nurseries' stretching from Park Avenue westwards towards the railway, ending at the eastern side of a free field which was later developed and is now Wilfield Road. The firm Jameson Robert Sons Royal Nurseries, Sandymount, was mentioned in Thom's Directory of 1927.

The area where this nursery used to be was developed for housing in the 1980s and Park Lane and Park Court are there now. There is still a free space on Wilfield Road that used to be the back entrance to the nurseries. Only a wall separates it from the western end of Park Lane.

DATA FROM CENSUSES

The 1901 and 1911 censuses provide information about the professions and occupations of people. This information does not state, however, where the work is performed. With shopkeepers, dairy men, butchers, etc., it can be assumed that they worked where they lived. Many seamstresses worked at home as well. Civil servants, bank clerks and commercial travellers would most likely work somewhere else. As for lawyers and accountants, they might have worked from home or from an office at another address. It could not be ascertained where the people working in the printing industry had their workplace. There were around a dozen such people in both censuses. Many tram workers lived in Sandymount because of the tram depot on Gilford Road and where formerly a locomotive workshop had been, railway workers and employees lived in the Railway Cottages along the railway line between the Dodder and Serpentine Avenue.

The censuses also report some more unusual professions, such as bog oak carver, cooper, corset maker, hatter, portmanteau maker, saddler and harness manufacturer. The portmanteau maker kept his profession from 1901 to 1911. The corset maker from the 1901 census, on the other hand, had become an accountant in 1911 and of the three brothers who had been bog oak carvers in 1901, the eldest had become a teacher in a technical school and his two younger brothers described themselves as jewellers in 1911.

SHOPS

It is highly likely that from the earliest times of the village there have been shops in the area where they are now, concentrated around Sandymount Green and its surroundings, radiating into Seafort Avenue, Sandymount Road and Claremont Road. The 1901 census mentions dairies, grocers, greengrocers and spirit merchants, as well as butchers and victuallers. There was also a chemist in the village. The chemist later passed the shop on to his son, who was well known for his medical knowledge. Many an inhabitant of Sandymount went to Mr Batt's pharmacy, where they could be sure of receiving proper treatment for illnesses, cuts, burns and sprained wrists or ankles. A visit to Mr Batt was easier and cheaper than a visit to a general practitioner and some people even trusted him more than they trusted the doctor.

In the early twentieth century, quite a number of inhabitants worked as drapers or draper's assistants, so it is likely that there was at least one draper's shop in the village and most likely more than one.

In the 1960s, dairy shops, butchers, bakers and news agents could still be found in Sandymount, but there were also other shops serving more modern needs. There was a petrol station on Sandymount Road, where punctures could also be fixed, and there was a shop selling radios and other electric appliances. A sweet shop had appeared halfway down Seafort Avenue; the building still houses a shop but this now sells good secondhand ladies' clothes.

Shops sometimes moved. The shop selling electric appliances moved across the road, expanded its range and called itself 'Domestic Appliances'. This turned into a proper hardware shop, which is still there today, though it has changed hands a couple of times. The premises where it had been originally was turned into a newsagent with stationary and tobacconist called 'Village News'. An earlier newsagent and tobacconist had been on Sandymount Green, run by the still well-remembered Harry and Lily Mapother, who knew everything there was to be known in Sandymount. Indeed, Harry Mapother was given the nickname 'Mr. Sandymount'. The shop is long gone, but Lily Mapother survived into the twenty-first century. The Village News also served as a post office in later years. Not so long ago, the building was torn down and completely rebuilt. It now houses a hairdresser's salon.

The range and number of shops in Sandymount today is surprising for a village of its size. The supermarkets, butcher, delicatessen, fishmonger, off-licence, hardware shop, ladies' clothes boutiques, gift shop, florist, book and toy shop, school and arts supplies shop, curtains and upholstery shop, antiques and paintings shop and the bicycle shop are all very near each other.

SERVICES

Samuel Lewis's *Topographical Dictionary* of 1837 describes Sandymount's service industry as comprising a loan fund, a Bible association, a savings bank and a lending library. There is still a bank in the village today, but the lending library has disappeared. Sandymount is served by the Pembroke branch of Dublin City Library in Ballsbridge.

Lawyers, accountants and clergymen are listed in the 1901 and 1911 censuses, as well as teachers, including national school teachers, kindergarten teachers, art teachers and music teachers. On the lower income level, there were messenger boys and girls in service, who were living at home, apart from the domestic servants that lived with their employers.

Ordnance Survey maps of the 1860s and 1870s show a Court House, but this building no longer housed a court anymore

Surround of the former public tap on the sea wall.

and was used by the Methodist congregation for their services before 1864 and also for public lectures.

In former times, there was running water only in the houses of the very rich. Water pumps put up by the township provided water for the public. Sandymount still has two of those, but they do not function anymore; one is on Sandymount Green and the other is on the Promenade just north of the Martello tower. Public access to water was also needed for horses, even after the time of the pumps. On the northern end of the sea wall, there used to be a public water tap. The tap has disappeared, but its surround is still visible.

A post office in Sandymount is shown on the 1907 Ordnance Survey map with the signature 'P.O.', denoting the building that in older maps is described as 'Court House' and even earlier as 'School House'. The 1911 census gives the address of the post office as 19a Sandymount Green. Later the post office moved into Village News, the newspaper and stationer's shop on the eastern side of Sandymount Road. After this shop closed, the post office stayed on Sandymount Road for some years, but moved across the road into the back of a shop that was in turn a sandwich shop, a stationer's and a soap shop until finally the front of the room was left empty. Without much warning, this post office closed 'temporarily' at the end of March 2015. The quest to re-open a post office in Sandymount is still ongoing in summer 2016.

Today, Sandymount has a wide range of services, including (in alphabetical order) an alteration tailor, a bank branch, a barber, a beauty shop, a bookmaker, a dry cleaner, three estate agents, a framing shop, three hairdresser saloons and several solicitors. The village has two medical centres with more than one GP each. There is also a plastic surgeon, two dentists, a physiotherapist, an optician and two chemists.

As far as animals are concerned, Sandymount has its own Pet Hospital.

The outdoor gym equipment that Dublin City Council has installed on the Promenade is a kind of health service as well.

CARE FOR THE ELDERLY

The Iris Charles Centre on Newbridge Avenue is a place for the senior citizens of Sandymount and Irishtown mainly. People can meet and enjoy lunch there on Mondays, Tuesdays, Wednesdays and Fridays at midday or participate in a range of organised activities, such as a bridge evening every Thursday.

There are several complexes of sheltered housing in Sandymount. The oldest is Brabazon House, which was mentioned in the 1911 census as 'Home for Aged Ladies'. In that year, it cared for eight ladies between 67 and 82, each of them deeming herself 'Head of Family', which is an indication of the women's independence. Even the 'Lady Superintendent' was 63 years old; the in-house servant was the youngest inhabitant at 54 years of age. The house is still a nursing home with sheltered housing apartments run by the Brabazon Trust of Protestant Aid.

Dublin Central Mission (DCM) of the Methodist Church runs Margaretholme on Claremont Road. This was opened in 1965; it was one of the first purpose-built sheltered housing complexes in Ireland. Margaretholme was modernised in 2013. It facilitates independent living, with the possibility of support, for people aged 65 and over.

Bethany House on Gilford Road near Lakelands is run by the Society of St Vincent de Paul (SVP). It was built in 1986 with financial help from Dublin Corporation. The ground was donated by the Sisters of Charity. The complex was renovated in 1991. It provides social housing for elderly people in need. The SVP has been granted planning permission to demolish the cottages and construct a three-storey apartment complex and seven three-bed townhouses. Until this new complex is finished, the residents will have to be temporarily re-housed.

Mount Tabor, beside Christ Church on Sandymount Green, is run by DCM, like Margaretholme. It was opened in 1998 and provides nursing care for its residents. The Presbyterian Church runs another complex of sheltered housing on Tritonville Close, the area where the old Presbyterian church used to be. This development was finished in 2001 and provides apartments and bedsits for fifty people, with care, including nursing, available.

Apart from sheltered housing, Ailesbury Nursing Home on Park Avenue, near St John's church, is a private nursing home which provides different levels of care, up to high-dependency Alzheimer's care.

4

SPORT AND
RECREATION

Sandymount has always been a great place for sporting
activities. For a village of its size, the number of sport clubs
in Sandymount is astounding. Within the boundaries of the
very extended village, you can avail of a badminton club, two
bowling clubs, three cricket clubs, three hockey clubs, two
lawn tennis clubs, four rugby clubs, a soccer club and a water
polo club.

Some of those clubs share a pitch. This is not surprising
as some of the clubs belong to the same organisation, like
the YMCA Hockey Club and the YMCA Cricket Club on
Claremont Road. The Railway Union Bowling Club shares
its bowling green with the Bank of Ireland bowling club,
which has its own pavilion. Opposite Railway Union on Park
Avenue, Pembroke Cricket Club and Monkstown Football
Club share both the pavilion accessed from Park Avenue and
the pitch stretching from there to the end of Wilfield Road with
Monkstown FC in residence in the winter and Pembroke CC
in the summer.

Railway Union was founded in 1904 as 'The Railway and
Steampacket Companies Irish Athletic and Social Union' to
'promote and encourage sports and games and other forms of
social and athletic activities among the staffs of the Railway
and Steampacket Companies represented in Ireland, the Irish
Railway Clearing House (IRCH), the Dublin United Tramway
Co. and the Grand Canal Company.'

Irish Railway Clearing House is credited with the idea of
founding this union of clubs as they had had soccer and cricket

clubs in the 1903 season already. Railway Union now has clubs for bowling, bridge, cricket, hockey, lawn tennis, rugby and soccer. Formerly it had a club for table tennis as well.

Of the sport clubs that still exist, Pembroke Cricket Club (founded in 1868) is the oldest, followed by Wanderers FC (1869), Three Rock Rovers (1893) and Shelbourne FC (1895). Three Rock Rovers Hockey Club and Shelbourne FC (soccer) moved away from this area some time ago.

SWIMMING

Sea-bathing
Bathing in the sea, or at least in seawater, became fashionable in the eighteenth century. A. Peters mentions in her 1925 book *Dublin Fragments, Social and Historic* that nearly 200 years ago it was said that the ladies of Dublin were remarkable for their dancing and the men for their swimming. Peter Somerville-Large (*Dublin: The First Thousand Years*) goes into more detail. According to him, there were different bathing places for ladies and men. The ladies changed in bathing huts. In England, these were on wheels and could be pushed right into the water whereas in Dublin Bay the ladies, after changing, had to walk past the women selling crabs and cockles on the strand. The men, quite a distance from the ladies, swam naked, which astonished visitors, who discovered 'swarms' of them in different spots on the strand between Ringsend and Merrion.

By the end of the nineteenth century, naked bathing was not the done thing anymore, at least not in the Sandymount area. Poorer people still swam in the sea while the more well-to-do went to the baths. Even those who could not afford the baths would rent a bathing box as it was not decent to change publicly on the strand. In the Irishtown area, the cost for a bathing box was 1*d*; in Sandymount and Merrion, where people had more money, the cost was 2*d*.

Cranfield's Bath

Cranfield's Baths were very well known. They were founded in 1791 and owned by Richard Cranfield, a woodcarver and gilder who lived in Tritonville Lodge, just a few steps away. He advertised separate swimming baths for ladies and gentlemen as well as hot or cold shower or reclining baths for ladies and gentlemen. His establishment is thought to have been the first in Ireland to offer warm seawater baths. In the 1901 census, they are not mentioned anymore. It took around one hundred years until the idea of warm seawater bathing was taken up again by the West Wood Gym on St John's Road, which has a 25m (82ft) heated seawater swimming pool in its basement, together with jacuzzis, a sauna and steam baths.

Smaller Baths

Cranfield's Baths were indoor baths, but there were outdoor baths as well. The 1865 Ordnance Survey map shows a 'Bathing Place' on the strand at Prospect Terrace with a 'Bathing Pool' which at high tide would be surrounded by water. The same map shows a smaller pool nearly opposite the end of Newgrove Avenue and another even smaller one halfway between the Martello tower and Merrion Gates. At Merrion Gates an interesting structure is shown: from the last house on Strand Road, a short pier reaches out to a pool that is depicted as if it is surrounded on all sides by more than just a wall. This structure is named 'Merrion Baths'. It does not appear on the 1907 Ordnance Survey map.

Merrion Baths

Merrion Baths on Merrion Strand, often called Sandymount Baths on Merrion Strand or Merrion Baths on Sandymount Strand, were built by Frederick Morley of 6 Strand Road and opened in 1883. The cost is said to have been £5,000. Morley was an architect and an engineer. He also was a commissioner of Pembroke Township. The original grandiose idea had been a pier 4.8km (3 miles) long; they finally settled for 109m (359ft).

The pool, which was surrounded by changing rooms, was 36.6m by 36.6m (120ft by 120ft) and it was divided into two. The part for gentlemen was 24.4m (80ft) wide; the part for ladies was only half that width. The maximum depth in the bathing pools was 2.7m (9ft). The baths operated daily from late May to September, from 6 a.m. to dusk. Each evening the pool was emptied and each morning it was filled again with water from Cock Lake, which was filtered through sand and pumped into the pool.

The baths were connected to Strand Road by a pier 107m (359ft) long and 4.25m (14ft) wide. This pier was constructed from cast iron as well as wrought iron and covered with deal planks. At the land end of the pier there was a bandstand where a band played every Tuesday and Saturday during the season from 7.30 p.m. to 9.30 p.m. Halfway along the pier there was a refreshment room.

Trams (to Sandymount Tower) and the railway (to Sydney Parade) had special offers, which included the entrance fee for the baths. This contributed to the immediate success of Merrion Baths, which had 33,000 visitors in 1890. It is also said that the pier was an attraction for peeping Toms, who would stand under it and try to see through the narrow gaps between the deal planks. They might have seen the occasional naked ankle or some voluminous bloomers – even that might have given them a thrill.

Later, the baths deteriorated; people began to complain about the quality of the water and the number of bathers fell to 6,000 in 1911. The baths were offered to Pembroke Urban Council for £1,000. As it would have cost more than £10,000 to develop them to a reasonable standard, the council refused the offer. In 1920, the seaward wall of the pool collapsed. The baths were closed and the pier was sold for scrappage. Most of the outside wall of the pool and some of the dividing wall between the sections for ladies and gentlemen still exist, but their stability is doubtful as some walls contain big holes. In 2015, a report suggested that it would be cheaper to take the whole structure down than to try to stabilise it.

In the meantime, graffiti artists have grown to love the walls. From time to time, the council paints over the graffiti, which just means that the graffiti artists get a fresh canvas.

As far as the former pier is concerned, the only thing that remains is a brick quoin of the entrance (northern corner) which has been incorporated into the sea wall.

Quoin of the former entrance to Merrion Baths.

SANDYMOUNT STRAND

The water quality of Sandymount Strand is monitored and
it is still possible to swim there, though at low tide you have
to walk or wade for a long time before reaching water that is
deep enough for swimming, but these conditions make it ideal
for children, who are often seen in the water there during the
summer.

FORMER SPORT CLUBS

Athletics

The Irish Champion Athletic Club (ICAC), originally named 'Royal Irish Athletic Club', was founded by Henry Wallace Doveton Dunlop (1844–1930) in 1872 in Dublin University's College Park, but had to move from there very shortly afterwards. It got its own grounds during its first year of existence in the Royal Park Stadium, which became the Lansdowne Road Stadium and is now the Aviva Stadium. The athletic club founded by Dunlop did not survive long. In 1876, Dunlop proposed to turn the club into a company to finance the expansion of Lansdowne Road. This led to a split. Partly to heal the split, Michael Cusack, later co-founder of the GAA, was made a member of the council of the club, but he could not prevent the club's demise. In summer 1880, the tenancy of Lansdowne Road was passed from the ICAC to Lansdowne Football Club and in December 1880 the Irish Champions Athletic Club was dissolved. It had not survived long, but it had gone far in its attempts to properly organise Irish amateur athletics.

Cricket

An early mention of a Sandymount sport club appeared in *The Irish Times* on 14 March 1864, announcing, 'SANDYMOUNT CRICKET CLUB. A meeting will be held at the Phoenix Hotel, D'Olier street, on this evening (Monday), at 8 o'clock, for the election of officers for the ensuing season.'

Obviously the club did not have a pavilion. Later that year, on 20 July the same club was involved in a memorable cricket match against County Wicklow Cricket Club, which was captained by Charles Steward Parnell. Sandymount scored 524 in the first innings, which, at that time, was believed to be the biggest total in England or Ireland. During this match J. Gilligan scored the first double century in Ireland.

Lansdowne Cricket Club branched off from Henry W.D. Dunlop's Irish Champion Athletic Club founded in 1873. Their best player, Jack Hynes, scored the only century on the Lansdowne grounds in 1884. He did not only play for

Lansdowne, but also for Trinity and Phoenix and was capped twenty-seven times for Ireland. Lansdowne CC disappeared in the 1890s.

GAA
Ed Grays was founded in 1886 and played in Merrion. One of the Merrion landowners, Baron ffrench, let more than one club use part of his land for their activities. Ed Grays was one of the clubs that merged into Clanna Gael Fontenoy.

Sandymount GFC started playing in 1903. The Pembroke Estate papers in the National Library record that the club leased a field on Gilford Road for four months each year between 1908 and 1912 and for two months in 1915. The club seems to have disappeared after that. In the mid-1930s, a Sandymount H. and F. Club appeared and played until around 1950.

Hockey
Three Rock Rovers Hockey Club used to play on Londonbridge Road, where they shared the grounds with Lansdowne Lawn Tennis Club. They still exist, but no longer in this area as in 1981 they sold the grounds to Lansdowne LTC and moved to Rathfarnham.

Rugby
Sandymount Rugby Club is mentioned in Leinster Rugby's centenary book in 1979. It definitely existed in the mid-1890s, but is not mentioned in R. Peter's *Handbook of Football* in 1880. It seems to have disappeared and been re-founded in 1913. Monkstown Rugby Club have a photograph of a rugby team with the caption 'Old Sandymount RFC (1913), Junior Cup Final February 1914'. The caption also notes the sad fact that two of the players in the photograph were killed in the First World War.

Soccer
Freebooters FC was something of a special elite club in the 1890s as only young Irish Catholic men that had been educated in English Catholic colleges could become members. In 1900, the club lost the Leinster Senior Cup Final match against local rivals Shelbourne FC. Their highest achievement was reaching

the Irish Cup Final in 1901, which they lost to Cliftonville FC. This was the first Irish Cup Final played outside Belfast. The club ceased to exist around 1910.

Tritonville FC were in existence in 1906, but it is not recorded when they were established. Their reputation was not the best. In 1906, senior football clubs in Belfast asked the IFA (Irish Football Association) to prevent Tritonville FC from entering the Irish Cup. One of the reasons for this was that Tritonville's players were described as 'simply too brutal'.

Tritonville FC played on a pitch that the GAA used for matches on Sundays. This also created problems with the IFA, which was based in Belfast, and in 1906 Ulster delegates brought in another motion that IFA-affiliated clubs that played on pitches 'on which Sunday sports or Gaelic football are held' would be expelled from senior competition. Other Leinster clubs helped prevent the motion from being accepted. Tritonville was still playing in 1912, but disappeared not much later.

Ulster FC is something of a phantom soccer club. It is mentioned in two publications, in the brochure 'Sandymount' written by B. Saunders and D. Bradshaw in March 1975 and in a talk by Kevin P. O'Rorke on 16 January 1985 (printed by the Dublin Historical Records). Neither author gives sources. No other mention of a club of that name in Sandymount can be found and no living local historian in this area has ever come across references to a club of that name, apart from the two publications above.

Shelbourne FC is a former club not in the sense that it does not exist anymore, but in the sense that it is not in this area anymore. Shelbourne FC, known as 'Shels', was founded in 1895 in the Bath Avenue area and took its name from the nearby Shelbourne Road. They won the Leinster Junior Cup in 1896/7, in the following 1897/8 season they reached the Leinster Senior Cup final and in 1902/3 they won the Leinster Senior League. In 1905, they turned 'professional' in the sense that at least some players were paid: the first player paid by the club, James Wall, got a halfpenny per week and game. They first played on waste grounds in the Bath Avenue/Havelock Square area, as did other clubs, but Shelbourne used these grounds only in their first season. In their second season they used a pitch on Claremont

Road and in their third season they used one on Park Avenue before moving for three seasons to Beaver Row, where the Riverview Leisure Centre is now. Sometime later, they played on the former Shelbourne Park Football Ground on Sandymount Road until they moved to Ringsend.

Table Tennis
Railway Union Table Tennis Club was established in 1931 and still existed at the golden anniversary of Railway Union in 1954, but it has disappeared since then and is not mentioned in the club history written for the centenary in 2004.

FORMER PITCHES

Shelbourne Park Football Ground
The oldest purpose-built pitch in Sandymount was situated between Sandymount Road and the sea in the area that now is covered by the houses of Seafort Gardens. It is shown on the 1907 Ordnance Survey map as 'Shelbourne Park Football Ground', including a small stand. This might have been the pitch on which Sandymount Cricket Club, and perhaps Sandymount Rugby Club, had its matches. Perhaps the two had an arrangement like the one Pembroke Cricket Club and Monkstown Rugby Club have; they co-own a clubhouse and a pitch, which sees rugby during the winter and cricket during the summer. Shelbourne Park Football Ground should not be confused with Shelbourne Park Greyhound Stadium in Ringsend. Both of them have been used and the latter one was even built by Shelbourne FC, hence the names. Shelbourne Park Football Ground started as 'Army Grounds'. It was later leased by the Catholic University Medical School as their sports ground. Even later, it became known as 'Freebooters Ground' after the club who played its home matches there. In 1906, Shelbourne FC began playing their home matches on these grounds as Freebooters went into decline. Even some time after Shelbourne became tenants, the grounds were still referred to as Freebooters' Ground by locals.

Other pitches

In the beginning of the twentieth century, Sandymount GFC leased a field on Gilford Road for a couple of months each summer, but it is unclear exactly where this was. Any club in the early days of organised sport would try to get permission to play on any free, flat and relatively smooth area. The history of Fontenoy GAC, for instance, mentions playing on Bath Avenue and the history of Shelbourne FC also mentions the Bath Avenue/Havelock Square area, but grounds on Claremont Road and Park Avenue as well.

Royal Park/Lansdowne Road/Aviva

The Aviva Stadium, the newest stadium in this area, was built on the site of a much older stadium. The Irish rugby temple, which was known as Lansdowne Road Stadium, started its life as 'The Royal Park Stadium', founded 1872 by Henry W.D. Dunlop for his Irish Champion Athletic Club, which later branched out into different sport clubs, of which Lansdowne FC and Lansdowne LTC have survived. Very quickly it became the stadium for international rugby matches, but was also used for other sports, including athletics and bicycle races. It had stands from the beginning; as a report about the opening ceremony in 1873 mentions a grandstand. During its lifetime, stands were built, enlarged, taken down and renewed more than once. It never was a thing of beauty, though from afar it did not look too bad. Probably the same can be said of the modern Aviva Stadium.

Lansdowne Road Stadium had a total capacity of 49,250, but only 25,000 spectators would be able to sit. As FIFA and UEFA rules demand that at international matches all spectators have a seat, the stadium had to be temporarily changed for those matches; on such occasions, it had 36,000 seats. As the north and south terraces, which normally had no seats, were open, it was relatively easy to follow a match in Sandymount as the roars of the crowd could be heard over quite a distance. This, of course, was also true of the occasional concert at the stadium.

Lansdowne Road Stadium was completely taken down in 2007. The Aviva Stadium was built to replace it on the same site during the years 2008 to 2010. It seats 51,000. The Aviva

Stadium is jointly owned by the Irish Rugby Football Union (IRFU) and the Football Association of Ireland (FAI). Like its predecessor, it is used for rugby and soccer matches and occasionally for concerts. Due to the way it was built, it cannot be used for athletic or cycling events anymore, as Lansdowne Road Stadium once was.

OTHER RECREATION

Bridge
Bridge, to some extent, can be regarded as a sport as it is a mental exercise and sport originally described any recreational activity after work had been done – or delegated. Sandymount now has two bridge clubs, one in the Railway Union sports club family and the other a very new club in the Iris Charles Centre on Newbridge Avenue.

Walking
Dublin City Council organises a number of guided walks as part of its 'Lets Walk and Talk' programme. A guided walk through Sandymount, along the strand or to the neighbouring villages, starts every Thursday at 2 p.m. from Sandymount Green. For those who prefer self-guided walks, Dublin City Council, in co-operation with Sandymount TidyTowns, has published a 'Sandymount Walking Trail, Map and Guide'. Strand Road and especially the Promenade are part of the East Coast '*Slí na Sláinte*', which has been created by the Irish Heart Foundation.

Of course anybody can just walk off on her or his own initiative; for instance, along the strand, where outdoor gym equipment, installed on the Promenade a couple of years ago by the council, afford people further exercise opportunities without the need for club or gym membership. The strand and the Promenade are often used for casual running, cycling or ball games. Of course, others go simply to relax on the benches, the grass or the sand.

On Sandymount Strand.

Socialising

Socialising is an activity that can be done on the strand as well, of course, and for those who find it too difficult to get up from the sand or the grass, there are a number of benches. There is also Sandymount Green, where you can sit down during your lunch hour or after work and let the youngsters play or just relax, reading the paper or chatting with others. The latter is an activity often evident in any of the cafés in the village. Later in the day or evening, people socialise in the pubs around Sandymount Green or the bar in the Sandymount Hotel, where you can chat over a drink or perhaps watch a match in the company of friends.

HOSPITALITY

With its quiet atmosphere and its seaside location, Sandymount became a fashionable residential area in the early nineteenth century and many a Dublin inhabitant who could afford it moved to one of the newly built villas and residences, at least for the summer months.

For a shorter stay, they could use the 'village hotel' beside Sandymount Castle, mentioned by John D'Alton in the early nineteenth century. Earlier still, in the eighteenth century, the Conniving House accommodated guests and, according to Weston St John Joyce, there was an 'inn and snack-house' at the end of Sandymount Avenue where it meets Merrion Road, called 'Bird-House'. Travellers sometimes stayed overnight at this thatched inn, not wishing to go on till morning as the Rock Road was notorious for highwaymen and robberies.

Now just a couple of DART stops from the city centre, Sandymount is still an excellent choice for a stay of a couple of days or even longer, especially for people who want to get away from the hustle and bustle of the city centre.

Accommodation is available in various B&Bs. At the time of writing, there is also Aberdeen Lodge, a private hotel on the quiet and leafy Park Avenue at the southern end of the core village. There is a much bigger hotel in the area too, now called the Sandymount Hotel, but earlier known as Mount Herbert Hotel on Herbert Road in the north-western corner of the village, near the Dodder. In general, this location near the Lansdowne Road DART station is also quiet, though it can get very busy when a rugby or soccer match or a concert takes place in the Aviva Stadium just across the river.

The names of hotels and B&B can have many different roots. Mount Herbert Hotel, a family business, had started in 1955 as a B&B with just a few rooms. It was successful and soon the family could enlarge their place. They started with just one Victorian house, but by now have bought seven of its neighbours and increased the number of rooms to over 150. The hotel also has a restaurant and a fully licensed bar. After sixty years, it still belongs to the same family and is now run by the son and grandson of the founders. In later years, the hotel owners noticed the guests' confusion about Mount Herbert Hotel on Herbert Road, Sandymount, and the nearby Herbert Park Hotel in Herbert Park, Ballsbridge, so they decided on a name change. Now, as Sandymount Hotel, there is no more confusion.

Another interesting name was that of the B&B 'Aalen', which does not exist anymore. When asked about the name, the owner confessed that she had no connection with this German town and had never been there. She had chosen the name so she would appear near the beginning of lists of B&Bs (e.g. in the telephone directory), which was important in pre-internet times. It is not clear why the lady did not choose Aachen, which probably would have put her right at the top of the list.

Restaurants
Again, the Conniving House, built around 1725, has to be mentioned first as it was well known in the middle of the eighteenth century for its seafood, vegetables and ale. It is not known how long it survived. The 1837 map shows buildings in the area where it must have been, but does not give a name.

Much later, there was a restaurant in Sandymount's Martello tower for a time. At the end of the twentieth century, Seafort Avenue housed a Chinese restaurant, but this did not see the turn of the millennium.

After that, the situation improved. First Browne's, originally a delicatessen sandwich shop and café on Sandymount Green, expanded into a French-style bistro; then the Italian restaurant Mario's was opened on the opposite side of the Green in what had been Findlater's shop until 1969. More restaurants opened, including Dunne & Crescenzi, also Italian, and the Indian restaurant Indie Spice. Between Mario's and Pete's, which is also Italian, a new restaurant opened in 2016 where Itsa4 was before. Called 'buckleup', it offers traditional and Eastern-influenced dishes.

All three pubs now serve food and one of them, Mulligan's of Sandymount, lately opened a restaurant at its back. Away from the village centre, Sandymount Hotel has a restaurant as well. And for those who do not want to cook but do not want to pay restaurant prices either, the solution is Borza's fish-and-chips shop, which has been run by the same family for over fifty years.

Cafés

Many years ago, there was a café in the Martello tower. Later, Thom's Street Directory of 1985 mentioned a café called Village Fare on Seafort Avenue at the corner where it meets Seafort Crescent (where the Chinese restaurant was later). After this café closed, coffee might have been had in pubs, but for some time there was no café in Sandymount.

Now Sandymount Road has a café again near Sandymount Green and two of the restaurants serve coffee, tea and cakes in the morning and the afternoon.

Public Houses

Some years ago, it was occasionally said that Sandymount only had two pubs because the Earl of Pembroke would not allow more. This cannot be true as the 1901 census lists four public houses, whose owners were described as vintners or spirit grocers or wine and spirit merchants. Those pubs were situated on Sandymount Green, Sandymount Road, Seafort Avenue and Strand Road. The 1911 census only lists two pubs, one in Seafort Avenue and another one on Sandymount Green, which was also a grocer's shop. This was the situation until the end of the twentieth century. In the twenty-first century, a third pub was added on Sandymount Road. The three modern pubs are situated at or near the places where the 1901 census had listed a pub.

Today all pubs have big TV screens, mainly for sport events, and all of them serve food.

5

PLACES, BUILDINGS AND TRAFFIC

Public places are parks, promenades, squares, streets and even some buildings. Public places can be big, small and anything in between.

SEÁN MOORE PARK

Seán Moore Park is situated on the border between Irishtown and Sandymount, with Seán Moore Road in the north, Irishtown Nature Park in the east, Sandymount Strand in the south and Beach Road in the west. The park is frequented by joggers and dog walkers, but also by young people kicking balls. The Irish Heart Foundation created a closed-loop *Slí na Sláinte* in the park. In its north-western corner, Seán Moore Park has a triangular green space surrounded by Church Avenue, Seán Moore Road and Beach Road. This green triangle contains the Irish Mercantile Marine Memorial. This memorial was erected in 1984 to commemorate the members of the Merchant Navy who lost their lives during the Second World War. At that time, many Irish ships were named after trees, e.g. the *Irish Alder*, so the memorial is surrounded by a variety of trees in memory of those ships and the seamen serving on them.

Cliodhna Cussen's work 'Gallán Na Gréine do James Joyce' (A Solar Pillar for James Joyce) was erected in December 1983

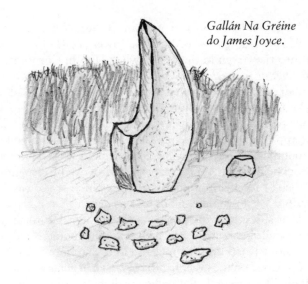

*Gallán Na Gréine
do James Joyce.*

at the southern corner of Seán Moore Park, where it meets
Sandymount Strand.

SANDYMOUNT GREEN

The amenities of Sandymount Strand and the Promenade have
been described earlier, but the quintessential green public place
for the inhabitants of Sandymount is Sandymount Green.
In Dublin city, 'The Green' might mean St Stephen's Green;
not so in Sandymount. The Green, our Green, was and is the
centre of the village. Despite the fact that Sandymount is one
of the youngest of the suburban villages of Dublin, it is the one
that has kept the tradition of a village green in its purest form,
complete with railings, trees, bushes, flower beds, paths and
benches. There is even an old water pump, though it does not
function anymore.

The Green has a bust of William Butler Yeats, sculpted in 1921 by Dublin-born Albert G. Power (1881–1945) and put into the Green in the 1960s when Dublin Corporation took over its management. On 8 June 2016, a bust of Séamus Heaney, sculpted by Carolyn Mulholland in 1976, was added to the Green. Sandymount Green is the oldest man-made public place in the village. It is older than Sandymount itself as it appears on John Rocque's 1757 map of Dublin and its surrounding area. At that time, Sandymount was still known as Brickfield Town. On his map, the Green can be recognised because of its location and its shape, which is not easy to describe. Most people think of it as triangular, but it actually has four sides. Its western side is not straight but forms an obtuse angle between the part between Sandymount Road and Claremont Road on the one hand and Claremont Road to Gilford Road on the other hand. However, in general, it looks roughly like a triangle both when walking around it, as well as from the air. Samuel Lewis is right when he writes in his *Topographical Dictionary* of 1837 that 'The village is very pretty', but he cannot be well informed when he then continues '… and contains many good houses forming a square, in the centre of which is an ornamental grass-plot surrounded by iron railings …'

The railings and the ornamental grass-plot must refer to the Green. The railings – surrounding the Green and not the ornamental grass-plot, as might be deduced from his writing – are still there and still the same, though the railings have accumulated many layers of paint. The railings indicate that in the beginning the Green was not a public place but, like many other parks and gardens, for the exclusive use of the residents around it. The Green was part of the Fitzwilliam and later the Pembroke Estate. In 1900, the Earl of Pembroke offered it as a gift to Pembroke Urban Council. The council described it as a diminutive enclosure that could be made into a welcoming place of rest and recreation for young and old, thus improving this part of the township. In the opinion of the council, it would become useful in this way, whereas before it had been 'only ornamental'.

The Green was opened to the public in 1904 when a water fountain was added. Unfortunately, this fountain does not exist anymore. The Green is surrounded by big trees, most of them chestnut trees. As modern gardening schools of thought move away from monocultures, chestnut trees that have had to be felled have not always been replaced by other chestnuts; instead walnut trees and a copper-leaved sycamore have appeared on the Green.

The Green is the heart of Sandymount. It is probably the most important asset for all villagers. Young families can let their toddlers play there without having to fear cars or bikes; older people amble around or take a rest on one of the benches, and at lunchtime people working in the businesses and offices nearby take their lunch to the Green when the sun is shining.

SMALLER GREEN PLACES

In Claremont Park, a development that was established in the second half of the twentieth century on the grounds of Claremont House, another small green spot can be found. It is not well known as it is at the end of a cul-de-sac. It consists of an oval grassy spot with some trees growing on it.

The smallest space that could be regarded as a public place nearly looks like a front garden. It is situated on Claremont Road, between Claremont Park and Sandymount Green, in front of the tax office. It is not fenced in and contains a life-size statue of a naked young woman stretching her arms out and looking over her right shoulder. The statue was sculpted by Rowan Gillespie. As there is no title or description, people are kept wondering about the possible meaning of a naked women in front of a tax office.

TAX OFFICE

The tax office itself is a public place, of course. Not many people in Sandymount know that it is there as it is not a tax office for Sandymount people. It deals with the corporate tax of Co. Wicklow. Only the Revenue Commission knows why it is in Sandymount and not in the middle of Co. Wicklow. But perhaps the amenities are better in Sandymount.

STREETS

No town or village can exist without access. In itself a street might not be interesting, but as soon as there is more than one street it becomes necessary to be able to distinguish between them. That is why streets get names, many of which have interesting backstories.

BIRTHS AND CHRISTENINGS OF STREETS

Most old streets started as dirt paths and developed first into a beaten track and then into a lane. In some cases, the word 'lane' is kept in the name for quite some time. The first Ordnance Survey map of 1837 still called Sandymount Avenue 'Sandymount Lane'. More modern streets tend to be planned by developers, like the Earls of Pembroke, who planned a proper street beside the sea wall – this became Strand Road. In some such cases, map-makers would predict this and showed what was called 'lines' where a road would appear later.

Even when properly built up, with houses on both sides, streets were not necessarily paved. Unpaved streets survived into the twentieth century, especially in villages. In cities and their suburbs, it was the coming of trams that brought road paving as it is easier to secure tram tracks in paved roads.

As far as names are concerned, 'Road' and 'Avenue' seem to be the oldest words attached to streets in Sandymount. The ancient 'Lane' had disappeared in the nineteenth century and only emerged again in the middle of the twentieth century.

'Square' is more often used in relation to the town centre, though the extended village has Havelock Square and Vavasour Square, both oblongs and not squares in the geometrical sense. 'Park', 'Drive', 'Terrace', 'Court' and 'Crescent' appeared later in Sandymount street names, like the renaissance of 'Lane', at a time when the last free spaces were filled with houses.

The question of what makes a street a 'Street', a 'Road' or an 'Avenue' has never been answered in a satisfactory manner. It is interesting that in Sandymount there are no 'Streets', but quite a few 'Roads' and 'Avenues'. In general, avenues are thought of as being lined with trees, therefore it is surprising that, though green-looking, Park Avenue has very few trees on public land, except for the last stretch near Sydney Parade Avenue; the green look is lent to the street by mature front gardens. Sandymount Road, on the other hand, is lined with trees for most of its length, except for the last stretch near the Green. At least part of Sydney Parade Avenue is tree-lined. On the 1837 map, it is not called an avenue – just 'Sydney Parade' – but then it probably did not have any trees at that time either. There were very few houses on it then. St John's Road is tree-lined nowadays. On the 1907 Ordnance Survey map, it only has trees around the church. The same map does not show any trees on Sandymount Road. Neither Newgrove Avenue nor Newbridge Avenue have any trees on public land. There are groves on Newgrove Avenue, though, and there were more in earlier centuries. Newbridge Avenue might not be much of an avenue, but at least it leads to the New Bridge.

STREET NAMES

As far as other street names are concerned, some are self-explanatory. The nineteenth-century Strand Road and the twentieth-century Beach Road are beside the sea. Sandymount Road and Sandymount Avenue are access roads to Sandymount village. It is interesting to note that the Ordnance Survey map of 1837 called the latter street 'Sandymount Lane' whereas Samuel Lewis in his *Topographical Dictionary* of the same year calls it 'Sandymount Avenue'. Tritonville Road always led to the area that has for a long time been known as Tritonville. Newbridge Avenue leads to what was at some stage the new bridge and is still called Newbridge today – or else Herbert Bridge or Lansdowne Bridge. Newgrove Avenue led to a small, early nineteenth-century plantation of trees, which thrived after the sea wall had been built. The 1837 map shows buildings called 'Beech Grove' and 'New Grove Seminary' on its south side. Some terraces on Newgrove Avenue bore and still bear their own names.

Other streets are named after people. Sydney Parade, Herbert Road and Lea Road all are named after the main developer of the area, Sidney Herbert, Baron Herbert of Lea. Durham Road is named after the Earl of Durham, whose daughter Beatrix Louisa married another Sidney Herbert, the 14th Earl of Pembroke. Leahy's Terrace is named after Patrick Leahy, a developer and councillor of Pembroke Township. Some streets are named in memory of what Sandymount had been before: a marsh with many willow trees. This led to the names of the residences Mount Wil (now long gone) and Wilfield. From those residences, the streets Wilfield, Wilfield Road, Wilfield Park and Willow Field took their names. Park Avenue was originally called Cottage Park Avenue and led from Sandymount Green to Cottage Park House, a Georgian residence that still exists, now with the name 'The Orchards'. In the early nineteenth century, Park Avenue was lengthened so it reached Sydney Parade.

Some names give one pause for thought, especially names that indicate an elevated place. The old Scalled Hill was such a name and even 'Sandymount' sounds as if the village should rise much higher above sea level than it does. This might be true for Claremont Road as well, if indeed it was named after an area and not, as is sometimes suggested, after the English country seat of Clive of India, who did not have any connection with Sandymount. Dromard Terrace makes reference to height twice in its name, as 'Dromard' is a combination of the Irish word '*drom*', meaning 'the ridge' (of a hill), and '*árd*', meaning height or hill.

An interesting name is Eagle Place. This short cul-de-sac led north from Seafort Avenue at the beginning of the twentieth century. It does not appear on the 1837 map. According to the 1901 and 1911 censuses, this area was one of the poorest in Sandymount. Its houses had two windows in front, between three to five rooms and many of them housed two and even three families. In the 1930s, these houses were demolished and better cottages were built. The name of the street was changed to Seafort Crescent. 'Seafort', like the longer and older 'Seafort Avenue', is another puzzling name. It definitely leads from the village to the sea, but there never has been a fort in the area. Over 100 years ago, there were buildings nearby called 'Seafield Cottages'. That name is much easier to understand.

Gilford Road and all the other names arising from it are the biggest puzzle: Gilford Avenue, Gilford Cottage (now replaced by a row of town houses), Gilford Court, Gilford Drive, Gilford Hall, Gilford House, Gilford Park, Gilford Pines and Gilford Terrace. Who or what was Gilford? Nobody seems to know. The fact that occasionally the word is spelt 'Guilford' or even 'Guildford' does not give us any hints about its origin either. The name appeared in the 1860s. By then, a road had been built that turned off eastwards from Park Avenue and led to Strand Road. This was called Gilford Road, but for some now unknown reason the first part of Park Avenue from the Green to this junction also was renamed Gilford Road. For some houses on this renamed stretch, the house owners refused to accept the renumbering and to this day have kept the numbers they had when their street was still called Park Avenue. Suggested connections with either Gilford in County Down or Frederick North, 2nd Earl of Guilford are very far-fetched. One source holds that 'Gilford House' stood at the corner of that road before 1840. The 1837 Ordnance Survey map does not show any building of that name. There is a Gilford House today at the corner of Sandymount Avenue and Wilfield Park, but that house was called 'Wilfield' on the 1907 Ordnance Survey map and the name Wilfield Park, which was given to the street that was built in the 1930s in what had been the house's garden, shows that the modern name of this house is quite recent.

How Bath Avenue got its name is not known. The street is quite old. In the eighteenth century, there was a lane from

Beggars' Bush Barracks to the Dodder. This lane went across the salt marshes through which the river meandered. When Councillor William Vavasour (1744–1819), after whom Vavasour Square is named, regulated the course of the river by building double banks on either side, that lane became easier to use. The 1837 Ordnance Survey map shows it as a proper street and on this map it is one of the few streets for which the name is given. Nowadays there are two suggested origins for the name. One involves the Marquess of Bath, who was at some time responsible for the coast guard and the lighthouses in the United Kingdom, which then included Ireland. This seems doubtful as the nearest coast guard station was in Ringsend and the nearest lighthouse in Poolbeg, both of which would have been easier reached via the lane past South Lotts and across Ringsend Bridge. The other suggestion is that it got its name, like Bath Street in Irishtown, because it led to the baths; its continuation Londonbridge Road and Church Avenue would hit Bath Street near the strand between Murphy's Bath at the Irishtown/Ringsend border and Cranfield's Bath at the Irishtown/Sandymount border. It is unlikely, however, that the soldiers stationed in Beggars' Bush Barracks would have had the time or the money to use the baths. The 1837 map shows only very few houses on Bath Avenue.

St Alban's Park is an interesting name in an area that has no connection at all with the first Christian martyr in Britain. The story of St Alban, however, might give a clue as to why the name was chosen. On the way to his execution, St Alban and the execution group had to cross a deep river. There was a bridge, but it was clogged with people who wanted to watch the proceedings. St Alban, eager to be martyred, raised his eyes to heaven and, lo and behold, the river dried out immediately. When he arrived at the spot where he was to be beheaded, St Alban was thirsty and prayed again. Immediately a well appeared. So the idea of water drying out and re-appearing became connected with St Alban. It is perhaps understandable then that the owners of houses built on an area that formerly held a lake and still has a high groundwater level would take him as their patron saint.

STREET FURNITURE

Of all so-called street furniture, street lamps are the most common and the most useful. Sandymount has quite a number of old street lamps, some of them over 100 years old. They were originally the poles that held up the electricity wires for the trams. Others are 'only' 80 years old, but are in a very decorative style.

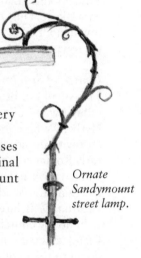

Ornate Sandymount street lamp.

Sometimes Dublin City Council re-uses street lamps in areas other than their original location. Any street lamp in Sandymount with the inscription 'R.U.D.C.' started its life not in Pembroke but in Rathmines ('R.U.D.C.' stands for Rathmines Urban District Council).

'LANES'

Like many other places, Sandymount has areas that are neither private nor fully public either. The residents call them 'lanes'. They are usually narrow and unpaved and lead from a street between blocks of terraced houses to gardens behind those houses. Originally they were used for the delivery of coal. In some instances, they were later blocked by garages. Some of those garages could only be used by the small cars of former times. With the arrival of the second wing mirror in modern cars, those garages became too narrow to be used and have been converted into garden sheds or sheltered seating areas at the end of the garden.

The lanes usually served more than one house, so they were not really private, but they existed to service a small number of houses only, which is why they cannot be said to be fully public either.

CHURCHES

Sandymount inhabitants worship in three churches, all in the core village. Only the two Protestant ones are on Sandymount townland, however; the Catholic parish church is officially in the townland of Irishtown.

Church of St John the Evangelist

This small but beautiful church at the south end of the core village was built on the suggestion of the wife of Sidney Herbert, who commissioned the English architect Benjamin Ferrey to design the church. The couple had seen and liked early Romanesque churches in Normandy and Sidney Herbert wanted there to be similar churches nearer home. In 1844, he had commissioned Ferrey to build St Nicolas' church in East Grafton, Wiltshire, in that style. When he then asked Ferrey to build the church of St John the Evangelist in Sandymount, Ferrey erected a nearly exact replica of St Nicolas' church, down to the gargoyles on the roof. The then Archbishop of Dublin did not approve of the gargoyles and ordered that they be removed, so the church of St John the Evangelist in Sandymount lost them while St Nicholas church in Wiltshire still has them. However, the dragon on the chimney of the vestry in Sandymount survived.

Sidney Herbert shouldered the full cost of the building, which came to £6,000.

The church of St John the Evangelist is not a parish church, but has a devoted community worshiping there. It was opened in March 1850, which makes it the oldest church in Sandymount. Like the community of St Bartholomew's in Ballsbridge, which was built by Sidney Herbert as well, the community of St John's is Anglo-Catholic.

Chimney at St John the Evangelist's church.

The stone used in the building was a soft Caen stone, according to the wishes of Lady Herbert. This stone weathers badly in Dublin's climate and expensive restorations are necessary.

The church has many stained-glass windows. The three in the apse are by Ward & Hughes of London and were made in around 1853. They are the oldest stained-glass windows in Sandymount. A window by Thomas Earley from around 1867 is one of the earliest windows by this Irish firm. Some other windows are by Joshua Clarke, who signed one of them.

In the apse, there is a beautiful mosaic (in two parts). The marvellous altar cloth was made by the Sisters of St John the Evangelist, an Anglo-Catholic order, which had their convent beside the church until some years ago. The church also possesses a set of art-deco plaster roundels of the Stations of the Cross. These were created by Roger de Villiers and presented to the church by Evie Hone.

Church of Our Lady, Star of the Sea

The Roman Catholic church of Our Lady, Star of the Sea, was built around a quarter of a century before Sandymount became a parish. It was built as chapel of ease for St Mary's church, Haddington Road, the parish church for the Donnybrook Parish, which included Donnybrook, Ballsbridge, Ringsend, Irishtown, Sandymount and Merrion. According to Bishop N. Donnelly's *Short Histories of Dublin Parishes*, there had been an older chapel in Irishtown which dated back to the time of Charles II. In the nineteenth century, however, this had become too small and dilapidated; the ceiling was propped up with heavy wooden beams and the walls bulged. The parish of St Mary's applied to the landlord Sidney Herbert to get a site for the new church. The request was granted and a site was provided that was big enough for a church, a presbytery and a school, all on the townland of Irishtown. This seems to have been important for the parishioners as the old church had been in Irishtown and the new church, like the old one, would serve all four coastal villages: Ringsend, Irishtown, Sandymount and Merrion. The ground rent was £10 per annum, which was a favourable rate.

To service the site, a new road had to be built; it led from Sandymount Road down to the edge of the sea. The sea then came up to a line between the old and the new part of the Star of the Sea school. James Joseph McCarthy, who had built many churches, was chosen as the architect. The building did not go up without mishaps. Around Christmas of 1852, a severe storm blew down the front and rear gables of the church before it had been roofed. Most of the cost for the repairs fell to the contractor, but some of the cost had to be shouldered by the parish. The church was finished in 1858 at a cost of approximately £6,000. The planned church tower, nearly 50m (164ft) high, was never erected.

With the splitting of the old Donnybrook parish into the parishes Donnybrook (Sacred Heart), Haddington Road (St Mary) and Sandymount (Star of the Sea), Sandymount became a parish in its own right in November 1876, at that stage still including Ringsend, which finally became a separate parish in 1905.

The Star of the Sea consists of a nave and two aisles of nearly the same height. Like Christ Church and the church of St John the Evangelist, the Star has beautiful stained-glass windows. The one showing St Columcille and St Brendon the Seafarer, one of the patrons of the church, is signed by James Clarke, the father of the famous stained-glass artist Harry Clarke. A bill of James Clarke Studios for four windows in the Star reads:

Order Book 1 Page 62 18 December 1912
Very Rev. C Ridgeway, PP Sandymount.
Chancel gable and side chapel windows as per estimate
17 December 1912
1 chancel, 1 gable @ £ 3.17.6 each £ 7.15.0
2 side chapels @ £ 3.7.6 each £ 6.15.0

The sum is £14 10s 0d or £14.50 in decimal coinage. Today's equivalent of this would be around €2,000. Considering that in 1880 Pembroke Township had paid the sum of £75 (the equivalent of €11,700) for the stained-glass window in the staircase of the town hall, Joshua Clarke's prices seem to have been quite reasonable.

Another window depicting the Holy Family is signed by Mayer of Munich. Comparing the style and themes of those windows with some of the others, it seems likely that at least three other windows came from the studio of James Clarke and four from Mayer of Munich. The newest stained-glass window is by the firm of A.W. Lyons & Sons, which had a studio on Westland Row in the 1940s and 1950s.

The pulpit and the communion rails were sculpted by James Pearse, the father of Patrick and Willie. Some of these disappeared with the change of the Catholic liturgy after Vatican II, but a part of the pulpit survives as a lectern, the legs of the pulpit now serve as the legs of the seat for the celebrant and parts of the communion rail are used in front of the sanctuaries to the right and left of the entrance door.

The esteem in which Sandymount parishioners held their church and the Very Revd Dean Andrew O'Connell, DD, the parish priest of St Mary's church, Haddington Road, who had instigated and supervised the building of the Star of the Sea, is evidenced by a collection for a Dean O'Connell Memorial in 1883. A list of those donors who gave 2s 6d or more has survived. It is touching to see that donations also came from people in the poorest quarters, some of them probably going round the neighbourhood collecting money for the purpose.

Detail of the communion rail by James Pearse.

Presbyterian Church of Sandymount
The Presbyterian church of Sandymount was situated opposite the Star of the Sea on Sandymount Road, at the corner with Tritonville Road. It was on Sandymount townland, whereas the Star of the Sea opposite is on Irishtown townland as the townland border runs down the middle of Sandymount Road. The church was designed by the brothers Hay, who were originally from Scotland, but later worked in Liverpool. They used a Dublin builder, S.H. Bolton, who was then regarded as one of the leading builders. The church was completed in 1858 at a cost of £1,600.

From around 1975, the Presbyterian congregation worshiped in Christ Church and the Sandymount Presbyterian church stood empty for many years. From the beginning of the 1990s, the Dublin and Munster Presbytery, of which Sandymount is a part, planned to demolish the church and build sheltered housing there. The plan also included selling part of the land to a private developer, who would build apartments for the free market. According to the church architects, the demolition was necessary because they had discovered dry rot. This decision angered many, especially as other architects did not find any evidence of dry rot. Still, the church lost its narrow steeple first and in 1999 was demolished completely. A complex of sheltered housing was erected in its place, as well as an apartment block.

Christ Church
Christ Church on Sandymount Green is the smallest and youngest of Sandymount's churches. It was built in 1864 for the Methodist congregation of Sandymount. Alfred G. Jones was the architect. Before its construction, the Methodists had worshiped in the Court House on Sandymount Green. In the beginning, the church had a simple rectangular layout. Transepts were added in 1872 and an organ was installed in 1909, according to the website of the Methodist Historical Society of Ireland, or in 1908, according to the *Dictionary of Irish Architects*. The entrance porch was added by George Francis Beckett, who as young man had lived on Herbert Road in Sandymount. Again, there is a difference in the year, as the Methodists hold that this occurred in 1911, whereas the

Dictionary of Architects gives the year as 1915, when the front of the church was completely renovated.

After the Methodist church of Ringsend on Irishtown Road and later the Presbyterian church on Sandymount Road were closed, due to falling membership, the church on Sandymount Green served those congregations from 1975, under the Alternating Ministry Scheme. In the beginning, all three communities (Sandymount Methodists, Ringsend Methodists and Sandymount Presbyterians) were named; later the name Christ Church was introduced. The building is a protected structure now.

Christ Church also has beautiful stained-glass windows, including one each by A.E. Child and Ethel Rhind and two by Evie Hone, all of An Túr Gloine fame. The windows by A.E. Child and by Ethel Rhind are signed. The Child window shows another sign, a kind of precursor of the Guaranteed Irish symbol. Evie Hone did not sign either of her two windows, but one of them shows its title, 'Rock of Ages'.

Christ Church also has a well-used community hall. It hosts many different events and serves at special times as a training place for the Epworth Badminton Club.

CONVENTS

Different religious communities have found a home in Sandymount. Apart from the occasional monk who helps out at the Catholic Star of the Sea, only one monk is documented in the history of Sandymount. It might astonish some people that he was an Anglican monk and perhaps also that he was a member of the Guinness family (see p. 133).

Sandymount Lane
The first congregation of nuns took residence in Sandymount in 1831. They were called in by Barbara Verschoyle, the agent of the Pembroke Estate. Mrs Verschoyle had founded a school for poor children in Sandymount and asked the Religious Sisters of Charity (RSC) to serve as teachers in that school. The school was on Sandymount Lane (now Sandymount Avenue)

and the sisters took up residence in a house nearby on the same street. This order is sometimes called the Irish Sisters of Charity or simply the Sisters of Charity.

The sisters called their convent the Convent of the Nativity of Our Blessed Lady. It had a chapel that was open to the public, but it was so small that the sisters themselves had to follow Mass from their parlour. The convent building does not exist anymore. It was directly opposite what is now the Enable Ireland School, but around 1900 or shortly afterwards it was replaced by a terrace of four houses.

Lakelands

Lakelands was built around 1800 as a private residence, which was mentioned by Lewis in 1837 as the principle seat in Sandymount. It did not stay private for long after that. In 1856, the Order of the Discalced Carmelite Sisters (OCD) moved in and called it the 'Convent of the Immaculate Conception'. Prior to this move, they had been on North William Street, where they had managed a school and an orphanage. As a contemplative order, they had hoped that they could leave both the school and the orphanage behind them, but their hope was not fulfilled; the school and the orphanage moved with them to Sandymount. In 1876, they swapped places with the Sisters of Charity, who moved to Lakelands. The Sisters of Charity took over the school of the Carmelite Sisters and merged their own school with it. The Carmelite Sisters did not stay in Sandymount much longer; they moved to Roebuck one year later. In 1998, the school was handed over to the parish.

St John's

The Community of St John the Evangelist (CSJE) is an Anglican nuns' order, which was founded in Dublin in 1912. In 1967, the sisters moved to Wales, but they came back to Dublin in 1996. As their original convent on St John's Road, opposite St John's church, had been sold and replaced by an apartment complex, they moved to Pembroke Lane in Ballsbridge. They were known as the Sisters of St John the Evangelist, which led to the following interesting anecdote in Sandymount.

Two nuns of the order went to the city in a bus. When accosted by a ticket inspector, the two nuns searched for the tickets in their habits, but they could not find them immediately. The inspector assumed that they had not bought any tickets. The two nuns were shocked when he accused them of fare-dodging. 'We would never do that!' they insisted. 'We are Sisters of St John the Evangelist!' 'That's a bloody lie to begin with!' was the inspector's curt reply. As no bad consequences are reported, the sisters must have found their tickets.

Dunroe

Dunroe on Gilford Road is shown on the 1907 Ordnance Survey map, already bearing that name. It is now the seat of the generalate of the Franciscan Missionary Sisters for Africa (FMSA). This order was founded in 1952 by Mother Kevin (Teresa Kearney), who then was 77 years old. Mother Kevin had been a Franciscan Sister of St Mary's Abbey, Mill Hill, London, since 1895. She went to Uganda in 1903 and worked there for many years. She founded the Franciscan Missionary Sisters for Africa for nuns willing to go to that continent. She spent the last years of her life in America to organise support for the order. Mother Kevin died in 1957. Dunroe is the generalate of the order, but the motherhouse is Mount Oliver in Dundalk, County Louth.

OTHER RELIGIOUS BUILDINGS

Gilford Hall

Gilford Hall on Gilford Road occupies a triangular site in the grounds of Lakelands. An inscription on its gable gives 1876 as the year in which it was built. In the 1901 census, it is described as 'Private Dwelling', but the 1911 census calls it 'Meeting House and Private Dwelling'. Since then the building has been used for offices. One of the firms currently using it clarified that Gilford Hall was built as a Meeting Hall for the Society of Friends (Quakers).

Gurdwara Guru Nanak Darbar

The only gurdwara in the Republic of Ireland is situated on Serpentine Avenue, Sandymount, in a building that was formerly a cinema.

A gurdwara is where members of the Sikh religion worship. Every gurdwara has a place where the Holy Scripture Guru Granth Sahib is placed on an elevated throne, called Takhat, in a prominent central position. Most gurdwaras, including the one in Sandymount, provide free vegetarian food. A gurdwara may also have a library, a nursery, a classroom and a community centre. Any gurdwara can be identified from a distance by tall flagpoles bearing the Sikh flag.

Sikhism is a monotheistic religion that originated in the fifteenth century in the Punjab. A Sikh, according to Article I of the Sikh code of conduct, is 'any human being who faithfully believes in One Immortal Being; ten Gurus, from Guru Nanak to Guru Gobind Singh; Guru Granth Sahib, the teachings of the ten Gurus and the baptism bequeathed by the tenth Guru'.

Sikhs are accepted in many states as an ethnic group. There are more than 20 million Sikhs in India and nearly a million in the UK, but very few in the Republic of Ireland. Most of the Irish population of Sikhs live in Dublin.

OLD BUILDINGS

Conniving House

The earliest well-known building in this area was the 'Conniving House' or 'Conniveing House', as it was spelled on John Rocque's map of 1760. This was an inn at the edge of Sandymount Strand. It was built around 1725 and was depicted on Scale and Richard's 1765 chart of Dublin Bay as a two-storey thatched house. According to the 1760 map by John Rocque, it was situated where Seafort Avenue meets Beach Road. In the 1750s, it was run by Johnny Macklean and renowned for its seafood, fresh vegetables and excellent ale. It could accommodate guests and was often frequented by scholars and fellows of Trinity College, who 'connived' there.

Today there is no trace of it.

Brickfield Cottages

During the time of the Conniving House, the brick industry in the area had been developed and there must have been places to live for the ten families that the 1766 survey found in Brickfield. As these, however, were at best wattle-and-daub structures, if not mere mud cabins, nothing is left of them. John Rocque's map of 1760 shows some buildings, but the correlation between his map and modern maps is not good enough to know what and where these might have been.

Roslyn Park

The oldest house still standing in Sandymount has been known under a number of names: Gandon Villa (after its architect), Ashford Villa (after its first owner), Sandymount Park, Sandymount Park House, Park House, Rosslyn Park and now Roslyn Park. Locally it is known as 'The House with the Egg Cup on Top'. It was built 1788/9.

The house was designed by James Gandon, the architect of the Custom House and the Four Courts, for the landscape painter William Ashford. Ashford left it to his daughter Anne in his will. Later, the house was owned by Ashford's grandson, a pharmacist and general practitioner, also called William Ashford, who lived on Serpentine Road.

In the second half of the nineteenth century, it was the home of Daniel Lowrey, the founder of 'The Star of Erin' music hall (now the Olympia Theatre). From around 1910 until the 1940s, the Dunn family lived there. The Dunns were well-known fish and poultry merchants. They called their home Rosslyn Park.

From 1950 until 1982, the building housed a girls' secondary school, which was run by the Sisters of the Sacred Heart of Mary, who called the house Roslyn Park. Roslyn Park was not the only building on the grounds. The second big house, for years known as Sandymount Park, was demolished when more buildings were needed for the girls' school.

Since 1983, the complex has been the headquarters of the Rehab charity, which restored the Gandon building between 1988 and 1991. It is a protected structure now.

Sandymount Green

Sandymount Green had – and still has – 'many good houses', as Samuel Lewis remarked. The first Ordnance Survey map of 1837 shows that the north-eastern and southern sides were completely built up, as well as the first part of Claremont Road facing the Green. Only on the western side can a few gaps between the buildings be made out. Two of the buildings have a description on this map: 'Sandymount Ho.' is what was later and until today is known as Sandymount Castle and at the corner of the Green and Claremont Road (south side) a building is described as 'School Ho.' The eastern neighbours of Sandymount Castle are shown but not named. The 1907 Ordnance Survey map names them as Castleton and Castleville and shows them as separate entities with their own, rather big gardens. On this map, all gaps, except one on the western side of the Green, have been filled.

Sandymount Castle was built around 1800 and in the 1830s it was owned by Robert Corbett, a stockbroker and insurance agent. Corbett remodelled Sandymount Castle in the neo-Gothic style, which was much en vogue at the time. The crenelated roofs of Sandymount Castle and its neighbours Castleton and Castleville were erected at that time. Corbett also landscaped the huge garden, which originally stretched down to Lakelands. This garden, or rather park, had a water feature consisting of an artificial canal with a bridge across it in the middle and a pond with an island at its southern end. Corbett populated his park with peacocks and other fowl, as well as with deer. The artificial canal and pond are still shown on maps in the 1860s but are not on the 1907 Ordnance Survey map, on which the former park has been divided into four parts. Now the gardens of Sandymount Castle are much reduced; most of the former park was developed in the mid-twentieth century, with streets named Sandymount Castle Park, Sandymount Castle Drive and Sandymount Castle Road. Some beautiful old trees can still be seen in the gardens of Sandymount Castle, Castleton and Castleville. The west side of the Green has houses that are also protected structures.

The chemist shop at no. 1a Sandymount Green, with its unusual and protected shopfront, is known to locals as 'Miss Milligan's', though Miss Milligan herself is long gone. The shop was used before and after her, but Miss Milligan obviously made a huge impression on the people of Sandymount.

The shop was originally part of the house no. 1 Sandymount Green at the corner of Sandymount Green and Seafort Avenue. The 1901 census describes it as a grocer's and wine merchant's shop owned by the Fleming family, with Seafort Avenue as its address. The mosaic in front of the door of 'Miss Milligan's' still shows the name of the original owners of the shop. The shop is supposed to have been a chandler's shop when the Art Nouveau facade was added around 1900 to provide more light. The 1911 census records it as no. 1 Sandymount Green, a grocer's and spirit merchant's shop.

When Miss Milligan ran it, it was a hardware shop. The Milligans lived nearby; the 1911 census records their address as 21 (now 22) Sandymount Green. William Milligan, a manufacturer's agent, and his wife Isabella had two daughters: Beatrice Sara, then aged 16, and Audrey, then aged 8. It could not be ascertained which of the daughters became the Miss Milligan of the shop.

After Miss Milligan's time, the former hardware shop turned first into a bookshop and then into an estate agent's. For some time now, it has been a chemist's shop. As this was owned from the beginning by a woman, it was known as 'The Lady Chemist' to distinguish it from the other chemist shop. It is still there and is still run by a lady, albeit not the same one.

OTHER BUILDINGS

Old maps show quite a number of bigger residences with names like Poplar Lodge (where the Seafort Villas are now). Those names sometimes change from map to map. Poplar Lodge, for instance, on Griffith's valuation map of the 1850s was probably what was called Laburnum Lodge on the 1837 Ordnance Survey map. Likewise, Beach Grove on the 1837 Ordnance Survey map became New Grove House on Griffith's valuation map. None of them exists nowadays. What was Tritonville Cottage in 1837 was Erith Cottage in 1907, before it disappeared, along with Erith Lodge, to make room for a big building that houses a car dealership now. However, some old houses are still standing.

Tritonville Lodge was built in 1796. It was the home of the wood carver, gilder and baths owner Richard Cranfield. Later it was said to have been used by Customs and Excise as it had a wide view from Ringsend via Clontarf, Howth, Lambey Island and Ireland's Eye in the north right across Dublin Bay to Killiney, Monkstown and Merrion in the south. The topsails of any ship could be seen up to 30 miles away.

Claremont Road was originally part of Serpentine Avenue, so it is not surprising that a villa-type house at the Sandymount Green end of Claremont Road was called Serpentine Lodge on the 1837 map. The house is still there, though it now bears the name Wilton Lodge and is easily overlooked as it is nearly eclipsed by its bigger and more modern neighbours.

Willfield, as shown on the 1837 map, is a complex of several buildings that in later maps and documents were called Willfield House, Willfield Lodge and Willfield. At some stage the spelling changed to Wilfield and in the twentieth century the biggest of the buildings, the original Willfield, became known as Gilford House. They are all still there, though Wilfield Lodge has since been rebuilt and modernised. Both Wilfield House and Gilford House (Wilfield) were built around 1800. Not far from them on Sandymount Avenue, but on the other side, is Connaught House. This is shown with the same name on the 1907 Ordnance Survey map while on the 1837 map it is called Adelaide Lodge.

On Park Avenue, opposite the grounds of Lakelands, is the former Cottage Park House, which gave its name to Cottage Park Avenue, now shortened to Park Avenue. The house is shown on the 1837 map but without a name. The 1907 map does not give it a name either, but shows it the way it is today, with a drive coming to its front from the gate at the northern end of the site. The house is now called The Orchards. Nearby, there was a house called Park View on the 1837 map, probably because the park behind Willfield could be seen from the back of the house. Neither the building nor the park are there nowadays.

Strand Road had Belvidere House, which is shown on the 1837 Ordnance Survey map. It was probably a family residence then, though in the 1911 census it was home to a number of families and today it is still divided into apartments, with extensions and an additional building beside it, also divided into apartments. Two houses on Sydney Parade, which are shown on the 1837 map, no. 51, 'Pembroke Lodge', and no. 53, 'Herbert Lodge', are there still, inhabited and in very good condition. Holyrood Castle, near Sandymount DART station, was built at the end of the nineteenth century and replaced an older building with the name Castle Kennedy. In 1872, Dublin Corporation proposed using it as a smallpox hospital. Not surprisingly, the project met with very strong opposition in Sandymount and Ballsbridge and was finally dropped in favour of a floating hospital near Pigeon House Harbour.

CINEMA

For some decades, Sandymount had a cinema. This had opened on Serpentine Avenue around 1936 under the name 'Astoria'. It had a simple, functional design and 700 seats. It was one of the few cinemas in the Dublin area that operated every day, including Sundays. In 1947, its name was changed to 'Ritz' and in the early 1970s it was changed to 'Oscar Film Centre'. Locally it was always known as 'The Shack'. In 1976, the cinema turned into the Oscar Theatre, but in 1985 the theatre shows also stopped. The building was sold, completely stripped on the inside and re-opened as the Gurdwara Guru Nanak Darbar.

THE CANAL

Before the railway era, bulky goods were transported by horse and cart. This was very slow as horses could only haul small loads and the roads were in bad condition. Even on a road with a relatively good surface, a horse could pull only 2 tons. The building of the canals improved the situation. Now horses could haul loads of up to 50 tons. The speed did not increase, but the improvement was noticeable. With the introduction of motorised barges, the speed improved, though not by much, especially when the route included locks.

At times when bigger ships could not reach Dublin because their draught was too deep for the many shallow parts in the mouth of the Liffey and Dublin Bay, the merchant marine had to use the harbour of Kingstown (now Dún Laoghaire). To get the goods from there to Dublin, a canal was planned as the Rock Road was notorious not only because of its bad state, but also because of robbers and highwaymen. This canal was to stretch from Kingstown northwards, parallel to the Rock Road until Merrion Gates were reached. From there, the canal would go in a straight line through Merrion, Sandymount and Beggarsbush townlands until it reached Grand Canal Dock or the Liffey in Ringsend. This canal would either have to be very deep to deal with different water levels caused by the tides or it would have to have locks, which would slow the traffic considerably. How the Dodder would be crossed is not clear. As canals built in those days were rather narrow, such a canal would not be of much use nowadays. Luckily it never was built because canals lost out against the more competitive railway.

BRIDGES

Sandymount needs bridges because of the Dodder. In earlier times, the Dodder could be forded in some places, but only at low tide. Fords that allow passage across uncontrollable rivers are always difficult. For that reason, there have been bridges over the Dodder since at least the seventeenth century. They usually did not last very long as the Dodder can be very destructive when it floods.

Railway Bridge

The first permanent bridge in Sandymount was the railway bridge near Lansdowne Road, but even this bridge has a history of being damaged by river floods. The railway was supposed to be opened late in 1834; however, before the opening date, the newly built stone bridge was destroyed when the Dodder flooded in November of that year. The whole bridge had to be removed and replaced by a provisional bridge, described on the 1837 Ordnance Survey map as 'Wooden Bridge'. As often happens, provisional solutions last longer than planned. This provisional bridge held for sixteen years, when a new bridge was finally built. That, however, was not the end of the story. Further destructive floods took their toll. The bridge was strengthened in 1884, but every so often damage had to be repaired. The last major work on this bridge was done after a flood in 2011.

London Bridge

Nobody seems to know how this bridge got this name. An early version of the bridge was built around 1800. A coloured drawing of it by George Victor du Noyer, held by the National Gallery, shows a rickety-looking wooden structure that makes one wonder how it survived even a minor Dodder flood. The bridge is shown on the first Ordnance Survey map of the area in 1837, but this map includes the comment, 'No Road on Br.' In 1857, a stone bridge with three arches was built. This bridge was strong enough for the double track of the no. 4 tramline later. Subsequent changes in the type of traffic crossing the bridge brought more changes. The tram is long gone, but the bridge is too narrow for modern traffic. It is still used in both directions, but now has just one lane and a set of lights to control the traffic.

London Bridge, Sandymount.

Newbridge

This bridge is also called Herbert Bridge or Lansdowne Bridge after the two streets that it connects. It is situated where a weir used to be when the Dodderbank Distillery was still working. The 1837 Ordnance Survey map shows that weir and indicates that a crossing of the river was possible there. The bridge looks very similar to London Bridge, which was built in 1857, but it is not known when exactly Newbridge was built. It is shown on the 1878 Ordnance Survey map.

RAILWAY

Until the fourth decade of the nineteenth century, anybody who did not have access to a horse or a carriage of any description could hire a hackney car with a driver. These cars had their approved stands and regulated fares, as taxis have now. The 1901 census mentions a car owner living in Sandymount, together with a servant who was described as a car driver. Those who could not afford to hire a hackney had to walk. All this changed with the coming of the railway. The first Irish railway was the Dublin & Kingstown Railway (D&KR), which ran from Westland Row to the newly built Kingstown (now Dún Laoghaire) Harbour. The idea had been that goods that came by ship into Kingstown would be transported from there to Dublin as Dublin Port was not accessible for big ships. The railway was easier and cheaper to build and maintain than the canal that had been planned.

As a goods line, not many stations would be necessary. In the first months, Blackrock was the only stop between Dublin and Kingstown. It became apparent very soon, however, that the railway's main income would be from transporting passengers and not goods. The company quickly adapted and more stops were built on the line. The railway company took advantage of the fact that many passengers wanted a cheap way to get to a beach by building a few baths near the railway line, including one near Merrion Gates.

Sandymount, Sydney Parade and Merrion got stops in 1835. Lansdowne Road was only served from 1870 on. Not all the stops were served all the time. During the 150 years between the first railway voyage and the coming of the DART in 1984, trains stopped in Sandymount for fifty-nine years and in Merrion for forty-seven years. Sydney Parade had been in use longest: for 104 years. Lansdowne Road was used continuously from 1870 on, most likely because of the RDS.

During the early years of the D&KR, the company had what was called a 'locomotive hospital' east of the railway, just south of the Dodder. This was not only to repair engines and wagons, but also to build them. When the railway company built a much bigger workshop south of the Grand Canal Basin (called 'Railway Coach Factory' on the 1837 Ordnance Survey map), the site that had been occupied by the older workshop was used to build cottages for railway workers on a cul-de-sac with the name 'Railway Cottages'. This address is of interest because of two signs.

The first is the sign giving the name of the street at the corner with Serpentine Avenue. In general, such a sign would give the name in Irish, the first official language of the State, in the first line. This is not so in this case. Here the English name 'Railway Cottages' appears on top and the Irish name '*Iostán an Iarróid*' appears beneath it. At least until 2016, it says '*Iostán an Iarróid*' on the sign, not '*Iostán an Iarnróid*', which is what it should say.

The other sign is a private sign. Cottage no. 12 has a beautifully decorated oval sign on its gate, with a nice bunch of flowers between the top line, 'Twelve', and the bottom line, 'Railway Cottage'. The address is, of course, 12 Railway Cottages. The owner clearly did not want to indicate that he or she owned twelve railway cottages, but just one, hence the singular.

BUSES

Buses first appeared in the Dublin area around 1850. They were horse-drawn and run by different firms. Sandymount was served by Wilson's 'Favourite'. Whichever firm, the buses were almost all double-deckers with a seat positioned longways on the roof. The interior, cramped and ill-lit, was used by ladies and the elderly. There was no smoking inside. Normally those buses were pulled by two horses, except for longer trips, if business was good and speed important. Under those conditions, four horses might be used.

Later rails were put down to make pulling the wagon easier for the horses; however, the vehicles pulled were no longer buses, but trams.

In the 1930s, Dublin's transport authorities decided to phase out trams and replace them with buses, which did not need a 'permanent way'.

In the beginning, the line numbers of buses were the same as those of the trams they replaced, so bus lines nos 2 and 3 went to Sandymount, with their terminus at St John's church instead of Sandymount Green or the Martello tower. Tramline no. 4, however, was replaced by bus no. 52, which came from city centre and meandered around the newer parts of Sandymount, with its terminus in Wilfield Park. This line was stopped in the 1970s.

Lately bus lines nos 2 and 3 were replaced by bus line no. 1 from Santry to St John's church, Sandymount. There is also bus line no. 47 whose route goes from Stepaside, past Belfield and Sandymount, to Fleet Street. In Sandymount, the bus routes follow the former tram routes and turn from Sandymount Road down Seafort Avenue, Dromard Avenue and Marine Drive to Strand Road and St John's Road and then back via Newgrove Avenue. This route is not easy for bus drivers as the streets are not wide and parked cars make them even narrower.

Another bus line that succeeded a tramline is bus line no. 18. Tramline no. 18 was built as the 'Rathgar to the Sea' tramline. It never reached the sea as the eastern terminus was at the kiosk at the junction of Pembroke Road/Northumberland Road/Lansdowne Road. When it was replaced by buses, the bus route was extended over the years and now goes from the Old Lucan Road in Palmerstown, near the Liffey Valley Shopping Centre, to Sandymount Green. To go the whole route takes seventy minutes. Sandymount Green, opposite Sandymount Castle, is not ideal as a terminus as on one side cars are allowed to park on the street, which means that any bus waiting there has to stop on the footway alongside the Green without leaving space for a pram or a wheelchair and sometimes, when more than one bus is waiting there, even blocking one of the entrances of the Green. For a short time, the bus went on to St John's church, where there is more room for waiting buses. For some reason, bus no. 18 does not go there anymore.

The private Aircoach company runs a number of bus lines from the airport, one of which (no. 703) passes through Sandymount on the Strand Road, with two stops in the core area and another one in the extended area, south of the Martello tower, on its way to Dalkey/Killiney. Sandymount inhabitants who wish to go to the airport can also use the same company's line no. 702, which runs to and from Greystones on Merrion Road, touching the extended village at the end of Sandymount Avenue.

On special occasions (for instance, during the Dublin Marathon), all bus lines with a route along Merrion Road are diverted through Sandymount.

TRAMS

To ease the workload for the horses of horse-drawn buses, rails were constructed for the carriages to roll on. These vehicles (invented in 1832 in New York) were called trams.

The first tramline to Sandymount became operational in 1872. It went from Nelson's Pillar via Merrion Square, Lower Mount Street, Haddington Road, Bath Avenue, Londonbridge Road and Tritonville Road into Sandymount Road. Shortly before reaching Sandymount Green, the southbound track turned down Seafort Avenue, onto Beach Road and Strand Road, on its way to the terminus at the Martello tower. Northbound, the tram left Strand Road at Newgrove Avenue to go to the Green, up Sandymount Road and back to the pillar. The route was popular. Dublin Tramways Company, who ran it in the first years, reported that in the year 1878 they had counted 1,175,896 return journeys on this route, many more than on the routes to Donnybrook or Clontarf. Only the Terenure route had more passengers that year. As long as it was horse-drawn, this tram used double-deckers, despite the fact that it had to go under Bath Avenue Railway

Bridge, which was quite low. This low bridge gave rise to a saying ascribed to Myles na gCopaleen that 'gentlemen on the upper deck of the no. 4 tram could not but be struck by the stonework of Bath Avenue Bridge'. The bridge was also the reason why line no. 4 was the last to be electrified (in the year 1901), five years after the electrification of Dublin trams had begun. After electrification it was the only line on which only single-decker trams could be used.

In 1900, another route was built through Ringsend and Irishtown. This route was electrified from the beginning. On this new route, double-decker trams could be used.

The tram depot for the Sandymount lines (no. 2 to Sandymount Green, no. 3 to the tower, both via Ringsend, and no. 4 to the Tower via Bath Avenue) can be seen on Gilford Road and bits of the rails are still visible, leading from the road across the footpath to the (now bricked-up) gate. The lower building, visible on the right, was built for horse-drawn trams. With electrification, a higher depot had to be built; this is the building facing Gilford Road. Cottages for tramway workers were built behind the depot, with bigger houses for the inspectors at each end of each of the two terraces. Both in the 1901 and the 1911 censuses, these houses had the address 'Tramway Cottages' and many of the eighteen small houses were home to more than one family. Today, as the trams have long gone from the area, the address is Gilford Terrace.

Line no. 4 was replaced by a bus in July 1932. Lines nos 2 and 3 were replaced by buses in March 1940.

BICYCLES

In the last decades of the nineteenth century, Sandymount was described as 'swarming with cyclists, especially of the fairer sex'. The title of this section is not quite correct, as the vehicles used sometimes had more than two wheels. Ladies used tricycles because their long dresses did not allow them to use the 'common' bike, known as the penny-farthing, and the so-called safety bikes, the type still in use today, were only slowly coming onto the market at that time. Cycling was mainly a pastime for sport and recreation, though the clergy and the police force used it as means of transport as bicycles were cheaper and easier to keep than horses.

There were many clubs for cyclists, both for sport and recreation, with groups going by bicycle or tricycle to picnics. In the Sandymount area, there were Pembroke Cycling Club and Sandymount Cycling Club, both of which accepted ladies as members from their foundation, something that was not at all usual at that time. A Sandymount resident, Sir Robert William Jackson of Newgrove Avenue, was for a time president of the Pembroke Cycling Club.

Today bikes are increasingly used as commuting vehicles as they are both faster during rush-hour traffic and easier to park than a car. At certain times, bicycles can also be taken on the DART.

PUBLIC *v.* PRIVATE TRAFFIC

From its terminus on Westland Row to Bath Avenue, the border of Sandymount, trains of the Dublin & Kingstown Railway and all subsequent railway companies crossed eight streets, all on bridges. Further south, the railway crosses five more streets in Sandymount, but on the same level, with the result that Sandymount has five level crossings. When the railway was built, the engineers had no idea how traffic would develop, so they should not be blamed for a situation that can be very frustrating. On average, a DART train passes every fifteen minutes in each direction, so the level crossings are closed for cars for an average of twenty to twenty-five minutes per hour. No wonder cars sometimes try to rush through when they should stop. Passenger cars mostly (but not always) manage this. When driving with a trailer, however, drivers occasionally misjudge the time needed to cross. When the barriers are damaged in such cases, the level crossing is closed even longer.

Perhaps it is good to be forced to have patience from time to time.

In the first weeks of 2016, new traffic signs were erected to point out that car drivers are nearing a level crossing. Those new signs warn that this level crossing is controlled by lights and barriers.

It has to be hoped that the new signs have the intended effect of getting drivers to slow down instead of crashing through the level crossing in the last moment – or even a bit later, as the case may be. It is interesting to note that those traffic signs show the lights, but not the barriers, and even more interesting that the trains depicted are driven by steam engines. Just in front of the railway line there is another warning sign, though, indicating that high-voltage electric wires are crossing the road.

6

INTERESTING PEOPLE

A number of Sandymount people are well known and others should perhaps be better known. Some of those people were born in Sandymount; others lived there for some time or at least had family connections in the village. Apart from well-known individuals, there are four well-known or even famous families with connections to Sandymount. Those families and individuals are listed below in alphabetical order.

IMPORTANT FAMILIES

Beckett
Samuel Barclay Beckett (1906–1989), the most important avant-garde playwright, novelist and poet of the twentieth century, won the Nobel Prize for Literature in 1969 'for his writing, which – in new forms for the novel and drama – in the destitution of modern man acquires its elevation'. He himself had no direct connection with Sandymount, but many members of his family had.

The Beckett family holds that they are descendants of a Huguenot family named Becquet. The first Beckett of which there is a historical record is James Beckett, a silk weaver who lived during the first half of the nineteenth century. This James Beckett had two sons, James and William. In the early 1870s, the two brothers founded the building company, J. and W. Beckett, which became one of the leading contracting firms in Dublin. Apart from running the firm, James Beckett (*c*. 1841–1915) was involved in reviving the Dublin Master Builders' Association in 1895 and was its vice president from 1895 to 1900, when he became its president until his death.

James Beckett was the head of the firm J. and W. Beckett and, after the partnership with his brother William was dissolved around 1890, of James Beckett Ltd, Builders and Contractors. He lived for the last nineteen years of his life in Riverside on Herbert Road. This residence does not exist anymore; it has been replaced by Marian College.

James Beckett's eldest son, James Walter Beckett (1875–1938), lived on Dromard Terrace in 1901. As a builder, he followed his father both as head of the family firm and as president of the Dublin Master Builders' Association. He also was a TD for Dublin from 1927 until his death. In 1911, he lived in Palmerston Road and later moved to Foxrock.

George Frances Beckett (1877–1961), architect, another son of James Beckett, lived with his parents in Riverside in 1901. He built many Methodist churches, including the now demolished Methodist church in Ringsend on Irishtown Road. He was also the architect for the porch of Christ Church on Sandymount Green. Three more sons of James Beckett were in the building business or became involved in it.

James Beckett's brother William did not stay in Sandymount but remained in the area. He lived on Merrion Road. His son William Frank Beckett was the surveyor for the Pembroke Library on Anglesea Road, Ballsbridge. He lived in Foxrock, where his famous son Samuel was born.

William Frank Beckett's brother, Gerald Paul Gordon Beckett, lived for some time in Sandymount and his children, Ann and her twin brother John Steward Beckett, first cousins of Samuel, were born in Sandymount in 1927. Ann became Ireland's first professionally qualified occupational therapist.

John Steward Beckett (1927–2007) became a musician. At school, one of his teachers had a great admiration for J.S. Bach, which he passed on to John Steward. J.S. Beckett attended the Royal College of Music in London and studied under Nadia Boulanger in Paris. He was interested in medieval and Renaissance music. From 1972 to 1982, he directed Bach cantatas every Sunday afternoon in February in St Ann's church on Dawson Street. On 22 July 1979, he conducted the New Irish Chamber Orchestra and the Cantata Singers in the Royal Albert Hall during the Proms. This was the first time that an orchestra and choir from the Republic of Ireland had been called to perform in the Proms.

Mulvany

The Mulvany family lived in Sandymount in the early nineteenth century, but the exact address is not known. Thomas James Mulvany (1779–1845) was a painter, a founding member of the Royal Hibernian Academy (RHA) and its first keeper. He later moved to Cross Avenue in Blackrock.

His son, George Francis Mulvany (1809–1869), was a painter as well and succeeded his father as keeper of the RHA. He was influential in the foundation of the National Gallery and became its first director.

George Francis' younger brother, John Skipton Mulvany (1813–1870), was an architect who built many railway stations. Apart from Broadstone Station near the Royal Canal, he built a number of railway stations on the Dublin & Kingstown line, including the former terminus in Kingstown (now Dún Laoghaire).

The eldest son, William Thomas Mulvany (1806–1885), was born in Sandymount. In Ireland, he is less well known than his younger brothers. William Thomas became an engineer for the Ordnance Survey and later worked as part of the Shannon Navigation project. He was a very conscientious worker and developed plans to give work to poor people during the famine. His superiors were not happy about that. Still, he became Board of Works Commissioner for Drainage and for Fishery. His suggestion that the drainage of the Shannon be improved would have increased the value of the land. Unfortunately, the landowners did not share his vision; they were too concerned by the fact that they would have to pay for some of the costs of the improvement. Mulvany and his superiors found themselves in front of a commission in the House of Lords chaired by William Parsons, 3rd Earl of Rosse, who was the leader of the group of big landowners opposing the work. The commission had to agree that W.T. Mulvany had not done anything wrong, but the damage was done; he had lost the confidence and protection of his superiors. He resigned from the Board of Works at the age of 48 with a pension of £675.

After retiring, William Thomas Mulvany got in contact with a Belgian-Irish mine owner and moved to Düsseldorf in Germany. From then until the end of his life, he was involved in the industrial development of the Ruhr valley district and became famous in that area. He owned or co-owned the mines Shamrock, Erin and Hibernia. None of them is in use anymore. He stressed the importance of the railway for marketing the coal and commissioned steam ships to take the Ruhr coal by boat on the Rhine to Rotterdam. He also suggested building canals to keep transport costs as low as possible. He did not live to see his vision come true; canals have been providing a cheap and easy way of transporting bulk goods in Germany until today.

He was made a freeman of the town Gelsenkirchen and streets in several towns of the area are named after him. Derek Scally wrote an article about him in *The Irish Times* of Saturday, 18 June 2005, entitled 'The Irish king of the Ruhr', but William Thomas Mulvany has nonetheless been forgotten in Sandymount.

Pearse

James Pearse (1839–1900), a monumental sculptor, was born in London. He came to Dublin from Birmingham around 1860. He had four children from his first marriage in Birmingham, of which two survived into adulthood. His son from his first marriage, James Vincent Pearse, was a renowned sculptor as well. James Vincent stayed in contact with his family even after his father had married again and lived in Ireland. James Vincent's grandson was the godson of Senator Margaret Pearse, the sister of Patrick Pearse.

James Pearse's shop was on Great Brunswick Street and at first he lived over the shop with his second wife. His two sons Patrick and William were born there. Around 1870, James Pearse and his family converted to Catholicism, but he always remained a freethinker. He worked a lot for and in Catholic churches and sculpted, among many other things, the communion rail and pulpit for the Sandymount parish church Star of the Sea.

For some time, the Pearse family lived on Newbridge Avenue, then they moved to 5 Georges Villas, now 13 Sandymount Avenue, in the very extended village of Sandymount. After the death of James Pearse, the family had to downgrade and moved to 1 Lisreaghan Terrace in Sandymount, now 107 Sandymount Avenue, where Patrick Henry Pearse signed the 1901 census form as head of family.

Patrick Pearse (1879–1916) studied modern languages and law, became involved in the Celtic Revival and founded a bilingual school. His younger brother William (Willie) Pearse (1881–1916) first ran the sculpting business after their father's death, but then got involved in his brother's school.

Patrick Pearse is known for his rousing speech at the funeral of Diarmaid (Jeremiah) O'Donovan Rossa in 1915. He was chosen as the spokesman for the Easter Rising 1916 and publicly read the Proclamation of the Irish Republic at the General Post Office. Both brothers were court-martialled and executed by firing squad because of their involvement in the Easter Rising. Their sister Margaret Pearse (1878–1968) was elected to the Dáil in 1933 but lost her seat in 1937. From 1938 until her death, she served in the Seanad.

Margaret Pearse, mother of Margaret, Patrick and Willie, was a Teachta Dála (TD) from 1921 to 1922.

Yeats

Three generations of the Yeats family had connections with Sandymount. For a number of years, some members of the family lived there and the Nobel laureate William Butler Yeats was born in the very extended village, at 1 George's Ville, now 5 Sandymount Avenue, just across the railway line. The Yeats family's connection with Sandymount started much earlier though.

The Revd William Butler Yeats (1806–1862), the poet's grandfather, married Jane Grace Corbett (1811–1876) in 1835. Jane Corbett's brother Robert Corbett owned Sandymount Castle and lived there. For some of his last years, W.B. Yeats' grandfather lived with his brother-in-law. The Revd William Butler Yeats died in Sandymount Castle in 1862.

His son, John Butler Yeats (1839–1922), also lived for some years with his uncle in Sandymount Castle while studying at Trinity College. Later, John Butler Yeats moved to 18 Madeley Terrace, also in Sandymount, though the street has since disappeared. He married Susan Mary Pollexfen (1841–1900) in 1863 and then moved with her to 1 George's Ville, where their eldest son, William Butler Yeats, was born. John Butler Yeats had studied law and was admitted to the bar in 1866. He started to work as a lawyer, but in 1867 he took up painting, to the dismay of his wife. The family moved to London, where John became a well-known portrait painter.

William Butler Yeats (1865–1939), the Nobel laureate, was born on Sandymount Avenue. It is said that when he was very small he used to be afraid of the deer his great-uncle Richard Corbett kept in the park behind Sandymount Castle. When his family lived in London, he spent his holidays in Sligo, which is where his mother hailed from.

W.B. Yeats was both a playwright and a poet. He published his first poems in 1889. He was very interested in Irish legends and the occult. Yeats was instrumental in the Irish Literary Revival and was a co-founder of the Abbey Theatre. He won the Noble Prize for Literature in 1923 'for his always inspired poetry, which in a highly artistic form gives expression to the spirit of a whole nation'. Yeats was the first, but not the last, Irish person to win the Nobel Prize for Literature. Many critics think that he wrote his best works after receiving the Nobel Prize.

W.B. Yeats was a nationalist, but not a radical. In 1922, he was appointed to the Senate of the Irish Free State and served as a senator until 1928.

He was attracted to Maud Gonne, who, however, married Seán MacBride. In 1916, after Seán MacBride had been executed, he proposed to Maud Gonne, who turned him down. In the same year, W.B. Yeats married Georgie Hyde-Lees, who was more than twenty-five years younger than him, but the marriage seems to have been a happy one. They had a daughter and a son.

WRITERS

Cousins

James Henry Sproul Cousins (1873–1956), poet, playwright and actor, lived in Dublin from 1897 to 1911. Shortly after marrying Margaret (Gretta) Gillespie (1878–1954) in 1903, he moved with her into 'The Bungalow' in Dromard Terrace. Both Cousins were friendly with James Joyce and liked his singing. They occasionally invited Joyce to stay with them, which he never did for long as the Cousins were vegetarians.

Gretta Cousins was very involved in women's rights movements and in this was supported by her husband. In 1915, the Cousins moved to India. James converted to Hinduism and took the name Jayaram. Gretta kept on working for the rights of women in India.

Seamus Heaney

Seamus Justin Heaney (1939–2013) was born in his family's farmhouse in County Derry. He was educated at the Catholic St Columb's College in Derry, for which he had won a scholarship. He studied English language and literature at Queen's University in Belfast, where he became interested in poetry. Later in life, he was a lecturer in different universities, including Berkeley, Harvard and Oxford. When, in 1976, he became Head of English in Carysford College in Blackrock, he moved with his family to Sandymount. He held the post in Carysford until 1981. In 1995, he was awarded the Nobel Prize for Literature for 'works of lyrical beauty and ethical depth, which exalt everyday miracles and the living past'. Heaney was not only a poet, but also a gifted translator and playwright. His translation of the Old English saga *Beowulf* is as famous as his play *The Burial at Thebes*.

Heaney died not far from Sandymount in the Blackrock Clinic. The last words that he texted to his wife were '*Noli timere*' (Don't be afraid).

Valentine Iremonger

Valentin Iremonger (1918–1991) was born in Sandymount. By profession he was a diplomat, serving in Sweden, Norway, Finland, India, Luxembourg and Portugal, but he also was a poet and a poetry editor. In 1945, he won the Æ Memorial Prize.

In 1988, he published a collection of poems under the title *Sandymount* but earlier collections (*Reservations*, 1950, and *Horan's Field and Other Reservations*, 1972) make many references to Sandymount and its surroundings as well.

James Joyce

James Augustine Aloysius Joyce (1882–1941) was one of the most influential writers of the twentieth century. All his works are based in Dublin, even though he left it for good in 1904. He had a good tenor voice and many of his early friends in Dublin liked him for his singing. He was also known for his heavy drinking.

Like his father John Stanislaus Joyce, he was a great mover, possibly because of difficulties with landlords, most of them financial. James Joyce lived in different houses in Sandymount. A plaque at 'The Bungalow' (22 Dromard Terrace) announces that Joyce stayed there on 16 June 1904. The Bungalow was then the home of James Henry Sproul Cousins and his wife Gretta *née* Gillespie. Some people say that Joyce did stay in this house in 1904, but not on 16 June; they believe that he did stay in Sandymount on 16 June 1904, but not in the Cousins' house.

In the same year, Joyce lived at 35 Strand Road and 103 Strand Road in Sandymount, as well as at 60 Shelbourne Road in Ballsbridge. None of these houses have a plaque though.

In Joyce's *Ulysses*, several scenes are set in Sandymount.

Plaque to James Joyce.

Thomas Cornelius Murray

Thomas Cornelius Murray (1873–1959), known as T.C. Murray, was born in Macroom, County Cork, and trained as a teacher at St Patrick's, Drumcondra. He first taught in Cork and later in Dublin. He was one of the great playwrights of the Abbey Theatre. He wrote fifteen plays, the first of which was produced in the Abbey in 1910. He was appointed director of the Authors' Guild, elected president of the Irish Playwrights' Association and vice president of the Irish Academy of Medals & Letters. In 1949, the National University of Ireland awarded him an honorary D.Litt.

From 1931 to 1959, he lived at 11 Sandymount Avenue, in the terrace of houses formerly known as George's Villas, near the birthplace of W.B. Yeats and next to the sometime home of the Pearse family.

Frank O'Connor

Michael Francis O'Donovan (1903–1966), who wrote under the name Frank O'Connor, was a librarian at Pembroke Library, Anglesea Road, Ballsbridge. At the beginning of his time in the job (1928), he took a room in Castleville beside Sandymount Castle. Later, he lived for a while at no. 57 Strand Road, the house that Anew McMaster and for some time also his brother-in-law Micheál Mac Liammóir had lived in.

Frank O'Connor was best known for his memoirs and collections of short stories, such as *Fish for Friday and Other Stories*. He was married twice and had two sons and two daughters. His second wife died in April 2016.

Annie M.P. Smithson

Margaret Anne Jane Smithson (1873–1948) was born on Claremont Road, Sandymount, into a Protestant family. She initially wanted to be a journalist, but in 1901 became a nurse. In 1907 she converted to Roman Catholicism and took Anne Mary Patricia as her first names. She became a republican and a nationalist and was the secretary and organiser of the Irish Nurses' Organisation from 1929 to 1942.

She published twenty novels and two short-story collections.

OTHER CREATIVE ARTISTS

William Ashford

William Ashford (b. 1746 Birmingham, d. 1824 Sandymount) came to Ireland in 1764. He lived for some time on College Green, but was invited by his friend Richard, 7th Viscount Fitzwilliam of Merrion and Baron Fitzwilliam of Thorncastle, to move to Sandymount, where Fitzwilliam offered him a site on favourable lease conditions and another friend, the architect James Gandon, designed a villa for him, which still exists. It is now called Roslyn Park.

Ashford painted exclusively in Ireland; his works include a number of landscapes in and around Mount Merrion, the Irish seat of Viscount Fitzwilliam, as well as twenty-four views of Mount Merrion itself. His paintings are mainly idyllic views of the countryside or the coast and the sea.

In the early 1770s, Ashford became a member of the Society of Artists in Ireland. This society ceased to exist in 1780. In 1812, he became president of the subsequent Irish Society of Artists, of which T.J. Mulvany was a member. After several splits in the society and some struggles between competing societies of artists, Ashford was instrumental in the foundation of the Royal Hibernian Academy. He was one of the three artists entrusted with electing the first members of the academy and he himself became its first president when, in 1823, the RHA was incorporated by charter. He is buried in Donnybrook graveyard.

His grandson, also William Ashford (1813–1892), was a respected apothecary and general practitioner in Ballsbridge. He was the tenant of Sandymount Park (now Roslyn Park), though he did not live there himself. He died in 1892 in his residence, no. 1 Serpentine Avenue. In 1893, a memorial in Irishtown was erected to commemorate his services to the poor of the parish for over half a century.

Richard Cranfield

Richard Cranfield (1731–1809) was a wood carver and guilder. Between 1765 and 1769, he exhibited sculptures and reliefs at the building of the Society of Artists, of which he was the treasurer. In 1766, he was elected master of the Corporation of Carpenters and represented this corporation on the city council. The best-known piece created by him is the chair for the president of the Dublin Society (now the RDS), carved in 1767 and still in use.

After retiring in 1797, he moved into Tritonville Lodge in Irishtown. He had founded and built the nearby Cranfield's Baths, which stayed in business for around a century. The baths were situated where Tritonville Avenue is now. Cranfield Place is named in his honour.

He was the grandfather of the portrait painter Thomas Cooley.

Shay Healy

Shay Healy (b. 1943), one of the sons of Séamus Healy, was born on Wilfield Road in Sandymount. He worked as a broadcaster and journalist, but also as a musician. He wrote songs, some of which he sang himself. For four years, he lived in the United States, singing in bars and restaurants. He also wrote a musical and a rock opera. He is probably best known for his song 'What's Another Year', the song with which Ireland won the 1980 Eurovision Song Contest.

SCULPTORS AND THEIR WORK

The Pearses were not the only sculptors in Sandymount; other sculptors lived in the area as well, even though nowadays only specialists will remember their names. Works of modern sculptors in Sandymount include a bronze bust of William Butler Yeats, created in 1921 by Albert Power (1881–1945) and put into Sandymount Green in the 1960s, when Dublin Corporation took ownership of the Green. Not far away, a bronze statue of a female nude by Rowan Gillespie stands in front of the tax office.

Sandymount Strand has two monumental sculptures. The granite monument 'Gallán Na Gréine do James Joyce' by Cliodhna Cussen was erected in December 1983, at the beginning of Sandymount Strand, in a corner of Seán Moore Park. The beginning of the Promenade is adorned with the sculpture 'An Cailín Bán' by Mexican artist Sebastián (Enrique Carbajal González, b. 1947), created in 2001 and donated by Mexico to Dublin in 2002. It was originally called 'Geisha', but was later renamed by Sebastián himself. For some time, it was known as 'Awaiting the Mariner'. Not everybody liked it and it acquired the nickname 'The Sore on the Shore'.

Sculpture in front of the Tax Office.

The most colossal statue is the 'Sandymount Line-Out' in front of the Sandymount Hotel on Herbert Road. This was commissioned by John Loughran, the proprietor of the hotel and a rugby fan. It was designed and executed by DS Art Studio in Beijing in December 2010.

PERFORMING ARTISTS

Gay Byrne

Gabriel Mary 'Gay' Byrne (b. 1934), also known as Gaybo, has been a radio presenter since 1958 and has been appearing on television since 1960. He was the host of *The Late Late Show* from 1962 to 1999. He was awarded an honorary Ph.D. from Trinity College Dublin in 1998, the Freedom of the City of Dublin in 1999 and a Lifetime Achievement Award from Irish

Film and Television Network in 2007. He was the chairman of the Road Safety Authority from 2006 until 2014. In 2008, he and his wife Kathleen moved from Howth to Sandymount Avenue, in the very extended village of Sandymount.

Séamus Healy
Séamus Healy was a civil servant and part-time actor in the Abbey and the Olympia theatres for nearly fifty years. He lived on Wilfield Road, Sandymount, with his wife Máirín Ní Shúilleabháin, who was a singer and writer of plays and stories, which she was fond of telling their six children, one of whom was Shay Healy.

John F. Larchet
John F. Larchet was born in Sandymount. He was Professor of Music at University College Dublin and director of music at the Abbey Theatre for decades. He also was president and musical director of the Dublin Grand Opera Society.

Micheál MacLiammóir
Micheál MacLiammóir (1899–1978), born Alfred Wilmore in London, insisted that he was a descendant of a Catholic Irish family from Cork. He was a great actor and impresario who, together with his partner Hilton Edwards, founded the Gate Theatre in 1928. His sister was married to Anew McMaster and Micheál MacLiammóir stayed with them in Strand Road for a time.

Shane MacGowan
Shane Patrick Lysaght MacGowan (b. 1957) is both a performing and a creative artist. He is best known as the lead singer of The Pogues, for whom he wrote a number of songs. He was also a member of Shane MacGowan and the Popes and Shane MacGowan and the Shane Gang, as well as working with a number of other musicians. For some time, he lived in Sandymount, but he moved in 2016.

Anew McMaster

Anew McMaster (1894–1962) first appeared on stage in 1911. Later, he became a theatre director and manager. In 1925, he founded his own touring company in order to bring Shakespearean plays to the provinces. He toured Ireland with this company until around 1960. For some time, Harold Pinter and Micheál MacLiammóir toured with him. Later, McMaster, who was married to MacLiammóir's sister Marjorie Willmore, played in the Abbey Theatre. He lived at 57 Strand Road.

Noel Purcell

Patrick Joseph Noel Purcell (1900–1985) was a stage, film and television actor and singer. He appeared in Hollywood films and regularly in the pantomimes in Dublin. For a while, he lived on Newbridge Avenue and for nearly a quarter of a century, from 1961 to his death in 1985, at no. 4 Wilfield Road.

Noel was a trained joiner and carpenter and had a philosophical attitude to life. When asked about an accident with a circular saw in which he lost his index finger, he explained, 'I didn't feel a thing. Of course it meant I could never play a violin again, but as I'd never played a violin in the first place, I didn't worry overmuch.'

Nine months before his death, he received the Freedom of the City of Dublin. Noel Purcell Walk, stretching between Drury Street and Mercer Street in Dublin 2, is named after him.

Arthur Shields

Arthur Shields (1896–1970) was an actor on stage and screen. For some years, he lived in Sandymount. His older brother, Barry Fitzgerald (born William Joseph Shields), won an Oscar in 1944 for best supporting actor in the film *Going My Way*. Arthur Shields fought for the nationalists in the Easter Rising and was for some time interned in Wales. He was called by John Ford to act in some of Ford's films, including *The Quiet Man*, in which he played alongside Maureen O'Hara and his brother Barry Fitzgerald.

SCIENTISTS

As three of the four Irish Nobel laureates for Literature (William Butler Yeats, George Bernard Shaw, Samuel Beckett and Seamus Heaney) have a connection with Sandymount, the village is often thought of as a place of writers. However, some eminent scientists have lived here as well.

Edward Conway

In 1932, Edward Conway (1894–1968) was appointed the first professor for biochemistry and pharmacology of University College Dublin. For his earliest investigations, he had to develop his own methods and instruments, which became standards for a whole generation of researchers. His explanation of the difference between the fluids outside and inside a cell laid the foundation for the work for which Sir J.C. Eccles, A. Hodgkin and A. Huxley were awarded the Nobel Prize for Medicine in 1963. From 1922 to 1934, Conway lived on Gilford Road in Sandymount.

Patrick Ganly

Patrick Ganly (1809–1899) was a geologist whose letters to Richard Griffith were illustrated with sketches of his work. Those letters and sketches prove that it was largely thanks to Ganly's work that the first geological maps under Griffith's name are so accurate. He was the first to explain the origin and nature of what geologists call 'cross-stratification' or 'cross-bedding', which can resolve the geological structure of intensely folded strata. In the years 1872-1894 he lived in Bath Avenue.

George Victor du Noyer

G.V. du Noyer (1817–1869), a descendant of Huguenots from Provence, was another scientist with an artistic streak. He was employed by the Ordnance Survey and illustrated geological, zoological and botanical specimens, including many fossils. He published numerous papers. In 1845, he lived on Seafort Avenue in Sandymount. The National Gallery has a coloured drawing of his, showing the first London Bridge across the Dodder between Bath Avenue and Londonbridge Road.

SPORTSPEOPLE

With the high number of sport clubs in Sandymount, it should not come as a surprise that some Sandymount sportspeople have become internationally renowned or have participated in Olympic Games, though some of these people are now forgotten. With the amount of cricket, hockey and rugby clubs (ten altogether), one might expect that these would be the sports in question, but that is not necessarily the case.

Ronnie Delany

Ronald Michael Delany (b. 1935), known as Ronnie, lived for some time on St John's Road, the border between the townlands Sandymount and Merrion. Ronnie lived on the Sandymount side.

Apart from being a member of Crusaders Athletic Club, which is based in Irishtown Stadium, he was a member of Claremont Lawn Tennis Club in Sandymount and won the Under-19 Boys Championship there in 1951. In 1956, he won the gold medal in the 1,500m race at the Olympic Games in Melbourne and in 1958 he won a bronze medal in the European Athletic Championship in Stockholm. In 2006, he was awarded the Freedom of the City of Dublin and in 2008 he was inducted into the Hall of Fame by Athletics Ireland.

Patrick Duffy

Patrick Joseph Duffy (1921–1987) was a well-known Irish fencer. During his young years, he had been a member of St Vincent's GAA Club in Marino, Dublin 3. He joined the Irish army in July 1940 as 2nd Lieutenant and during his army time he was introduced to fencing. The Curragh Military Fencing Club was instructed by French masters and under their tutelage Duffy became outstanding in this sport. He resigned from the army in 1946 with glowing recommendations. From 1947 to 1952, he was Irish All Weapons Champion and represented Ireland at the Olympic Games in 1948 (London) and 1952 (Helsinki). After the Helsinki Games, he turned professional, qualified as a *maître d'armes* and became a member of the German, as well as the French, Academy of Arms. In 1952, he founded the Salle d'Armes Duffy, for which he later bought the former parish hall of St John the Evangelist. Duffy ran training courses, including for the Finnish Olympic fencing team 1959/60. He was a member of the International Academy of Arms and founded the Irish Academy of Arms in 1952. His wife Shirley, also an extremely good fencer, participated in the 1960 Olympic Games in Rome as one of only two women on the Irish team. After Patrick's death, Shirley continued teaching fencing in the Salle d'Armes Duffy until 2007.

Mecredy Sr and Jr

Richard James Patrick Mecredy (1861–1924) and his son Dr Ralph Jack Richard Mecredy (1888–1968) were both well-known cyclists in their time. Mecredy Sr is regarded as the inventor of bicycle polo as he wrote the first rules for it. His son Ralph Jack Richard studied at Trinity College, where he was involved in cycling as well as field and track events, winning competitions in both disciplines. He lived for some time on Gilford Road where in the 1911 census he described himself as the head of the family, a medical student, aged 22¾ and gave his religion as Buddhist.

He participated in the 1912 Summer Olympics in Stockholm as a cyclist in the British team 'Ireland 3'.

Mecredy Jr studied at the Battle Creek Sanatorium in Michigan from 1913 to 1915. In 1915, he was on board the *Lusitania* when the ship was torpedoed. Realising that the ship was sinking, he got a lifebelt from his cabin as the supply on deck had run out and, after some consideration about the best escape route, he climbed down a rope from the stern of the ship and managed to swim to a lifeboat.

James Cecil Parke

James Cecil Parke (1881–1946) was an all-round sportsman. He played rugby for Monkstown, Leinster and Ireland (twenty caps). He also played golf for Ireland in 1906 and two years later won an Olympic silver medal in 1908 (for the UK) in the Men's Doubles in tennis. In 1912 and 1914, he won the Wimbledon Mixed Doubles final. He was also an excellent sprinter, cricketer and chess player.

Joshua Pim

Joshua Pim (1869–1942), FRCSI, was world no. 1 amateur tennis player in his time. He played for the tennis club that had been founded by Henry W.D. Dunlop as All Ireland Lawn Tennis Club, but later took the name by which it is still known: Lansdowne Lawn Tennis Club. Pim won a few times at Wimbledon: the single in 1893 and 1894 and the double together with his clubmate Frank Stoker in 1890 and 1893. He was also a keen swimmer and golfer.

Frank Stoker

Frank Owen Stoker (1867–1939), a cousin of the writer Bram Stoker, was a member of Lansdowne Lawn Tennis Club and won the men's doubles in Wimbledon in 1890 and 1893, together with Joshua Pim, also of Lansdowne LTC. On top of that, he was capped five times for Ireland in rugby.

There are a number of sportspeople still living in Sandymount or who are members of Sandymount sports clubs who have participated in Olympic Games or were capped for Ireland in international matches, at least one of them in two different sports: Kenny Carroll of Railway Union was capped for Ireland both in cricket and in hockey.

OTHER INTERESTING PEOPLE

Mother Mary Aikenhead

Mother Mary Aikenhead (1787–1858) was born in Cork of a Protestant father and a Catholic mother. Her father converted to Roman Catholicism on his deathbed in 1801. Mary, who had been baptised as an Anglican but had been brought up during her first six years by a devout Catholic family, converted six months later.

She belonged to the well-to-do middle class but from early on started to care for the poor. Through a common friend, she met Dr Daniel Murray, later Archbishop of Dublin, who talked about his hope for a nuns' order that would look after the destitute. The idea took hold in Mary Aikenhead's mind and in 1815 she founded the Religious Sisters of Charity (RSC), an order in which the nuns did not stay in their convent, as was the case with most other nuns' orders then, but went out to help the sick and the poor.

Mother Mary Aikenhead also founded St Vincent's Hospital and Harold's Cross Hospice, where she finally died herself. Barbara Verschoyle, the agent for the Pembroke Estate, asked the Sisters of Charity to run a school for poor children she had founded in Sandymount. Mother Mary agreed and in 1831 founded the Convent of the Nativity of Our Blessed Lady, a small convent on Sandymount Lane (now Sandymount Avenue) near the school. For some time, she herself lived in that convent.

Mother Mary Aikenhead became an invalid in 1831 and ruled the congregation by pen from then on until her death in Harold's Cross in 1858.

While living in Sandymount, Mother Mary wrote a moving letter about the poverty in the area in 1833 (before the famine) in answer to the 'Queries for Parishes in Large Towns'. She was very worried by the fact that the bad situation for destitute locals was made much worse by cholera outbreaks from 1832 on.

Leopold Bloom

Leopold Bloom (b. 1866, date of death unknown) is arguably the best-known 'interesting person' that never lived. He was not an inhabitant of Sandymount, but he visited the village. He became well known when another person with connections to Sandymount wrote a report of just one day in the life of Leopold Bloom. This report is nearly 1,000 pages long, the day in question is 16 June 1904 and the writer of the report was James Joyce. On that day in June, Leopold Bloom visits Sandymount twice, first in the morning to attend the funeral of a Sandymount citizen. Much later in the day, on his second visit, he sits on the strand behind the Church of Our Lady, Star of the Sea, which at that stage was still situated right beside the strand. There he watches a young girl with growing excitement. While he is sitting there, he hears hymns being sung and smells the incense through the open windows of the church at benediction.

View of the Church of Our Lady, Star of the Sea, 1884.

In reality, the windows at the east end of that church cannot be opened.

In honour of Leopold Bloom, every 16 June is Bloom's Day, at least in Dublin.

William R.F. Collis

Dr William Robert Fitzgerald Collis (1900–1975) was a well-known doctor who specialised in paediatrics and became interested in cerebral palsy. He was the director of the department of paediatrics at the Rotunda Hospital in 1932 and a physician at the National Children's Hospital (1932–1957). From 1957, he was head of paediatrics at the University of Ibadan, Nigeria, for nearly ten years and wrote books on his experience. After the Second World War, he was among the first doctors to enter the concentration camp in Belsen and led relief work on behalf of the child victims.

In 1948, he founded Cerebral Palsy Ireland (CPI) and in 1952 he established a school for sufferers from cerebral palsy in Sandymount, which occasionally had Christie Brown, the author of the book *My Left Foot*, as a pupil. The National Association for Cerebral Palsy, as CPI was called from 1952 on, moved to Sandymount in 1953.

Apart from his medical work, Collis was a member of the national Irish rugby team from 1924 to 1926. He also wrote two plays, which were successfully produced in Dublin.

Robert Corbett

Robert Corbett was a stockbroker and insurance agent who became a life member of the RDS in 1835. He lived in Sandymount Castle, which he remodelled and enlarged.

His sister had married Revd William Butler Yeats, the grandfather of the poet William Butler Yeats. His sister and brother-in-law stayed for some time with him in Sandymount Castle and so did his nephew, the painter John Butler Yeats, while he attended Trinity College.

Later Corbett's financial situation deteriorated, possibly because he had put too much money into the refurbishment of Sandymount Castle and its park. He had to sell the castle and park, became bankrupt and in 1870 committed suicide by jumping off the mailboat. He was struck off the RDS membership list in the same year.

It is likely that the Corbett family built the railings around Sandymount Green, but they are probably not responsible for the old chestnut trees around the Green. It is more likely that these trees were planted at the beginning of the twentieth century.

Edward Ennis

According to the 1901 and the 1911 censuses, Edward Ennis of 5 Dromard Avenue was a 'chimney cleaner' like his father. He was accidentally killed while watching the crossfire on the railway somewhere near Bath Avenue Bridge during the Easter Rising in 1916. Ennis Grove, off Londonbridge Road, is named after him. An older sign gives the name in Irish as '*Garrán Uí Aomghusa*', which includes a spelling error as it should be '*Garrán Uí Aonghusa*'.

'Ó hAonghusa' is the Irish version of the family name Ennis (as well as that of the family names Guinness, Magennis and Hennessy). A newer sign reads '*Garrán na hInse*'. This takes 'Ennis' as the name of the county town of County Clare. It was obviously forgotten that the street was named after Edward Ennis. The newest official Irish version of the name of this street is '*Garrán Inse*'.

Robert William Jackson

Robert William Jackson, CB, LKQCP, FRCSI (b. 1827 Edenderry, Kings County (Offaly), d. 1921 Sandymount) entered the army in 1854 as assistant-surgeon and served in the Crimea, during the Indian Mutiny and the Ashanti war, as well as in South Africa and Egypt. He was mentioned in dispatches, received a number of medals and was knighted. He retired as deputy surgeon-general. The abbreviations after his name mean: CB = Companion of the Most Honourable Military Order of Bath; LKQCP = Licentiate of the King's and Queen's College of Physicians (Ireland); FRCSI = Fellow of the Royal College of Surgeons of Ireland.

Sir Robert spent his last years in Sandymount, where he took a great interest in local affairs. He served for some time as chairman of Pembroke Urban District Council and also as president of the Pembroke Cycling Club. He had a daughter and three sons and lived on Newgrove Avenue, possibly in the house that is called 'Beech Grove' on the 1837 map and 'New Grove House' on the 1907 map. This building does not exist anymore; it has been replaced by the apartment block of St Cathryn's Court.

McDermott & McGough

The Americans David McDermott (b. 1952) and Peter McGough (b. 1958) are rather eccentric visual artists who occasionally pretend to live in bygone times. In Sandymount, they rented an Edwardian house on Sandymount Avenue and changed its interior and its garden into what they thought it had looked like when it was built, down to the dogs and chicken in the garden. In the front garden, they erected a kind of headstone with the inscription, 'The discoverers of de-aging and life everlasting 1886 McDermott and McGough'. They then photographed the results and showed the photographs in exhibitions. After fifteen years at 26 Sandymount Avenue, they were evicted, as they had been from other houses in the past. They never thought of asking house owners for permission to make their sometimes considerable alterations. Older people still remember at least one of them riding a 'High Nellie' through Sandymount in old-fashioned clothes. The headstone in the front garden has been removed; the house has stood empty for many years.

John MacNamara

John MacNamara (*c.* 1764–1822) was an Irish scholar and collector of manuscripts. He was a native Irish speaker from Clare. He was involved in the short-lived Gaelic Society and then in the equally short-lived Iberno-Celtic Society. For health reasons, he moved to Sandymount in 1814 and died there in 1822. He is buried in St Matthew's in Irishtown. After his death, his valuable manuscripts were sold, but in bits and pieces and not as a collection, unfortunately.

James Stephens

James Stephens (1825–1901) was the co-founder of what was later named the Irish Republican Brotherhood (IRB). As a nationalist and a republican, he was constantly in conflict with the authorities and could not always use his own name. In 1865, he rented 'Fairfield', a house on Newbridge Avenue, under the name Revd Mr Herbert of Killarney. Three other gentlemen stayed in the house with this reverend. A few months later, the house was surrounded by police, the four gentlemen, including the reverend, were arrested and taken to Richmond Jail. Only then did the owner of the house learn the real name of his tenant. Nine days after his arrest, Stephens escaped to France with the help of a warder and some friends outside the jail. He is buried in Glasnevin.

Barbara Verschoyle

Barbara Verschoyle (1752–1837), *née* Fagan, worked as the agent for three different landlords. Her parents Bryan and Elizabeth Fagan had been agents for the 6th and 7th Viscounts Fitzwilliam of Merrion. Bryan died in 1761 and Elizabeth, who after her husband's death served as sole agent for the 7th Viscount, died in 1789. Their daughter Barbara succeeded her as agent for the 7th Viscount. After Viscount Fitzwilliam's death in 1816, she stayed on as agent for the new owner, the 11th Earl of Pembroke, and after him his son Sidney Herbert.

The Fagans were Catholics, but Barbara married the Protestant Richard Verschoyle (1751–1827). They had no children. They were both active in their respective Churches; Richard was church warden in Taney parish (Dundrum) for some years, whereas Barbara got the 7th Viscount Fitzwilliam to build a new Catholic church in Booterstown.

Barbara also organised a school for poor children on Sandymount Lane (now Sandymount Avenue). To run the school, she called on the Sisters of Charity, who later exchanged their abode with the Carmelite Sisters and moved to Lakelands. Barbara Verschoyle presented the Sisters of Charity with a golden chalice for their chapel with the inscription '*Donum Barbarae Verschoyle Conventus Sororum Charitatis Sandymount Fundatricis A.D. 1831. Orate pro ea.*' (A present of Barbara Verschoyle, the foundress of the Convent of the Sisters of Charity A.D. 1831. Pray for her.) This chalice is no longer in Sandymount as the sisters have passed it on to a mission station in Africa.

Dublin City has honoured the Verschoyles by naming Verschoyle Place (between Merrion Square East and the Grand Canal) after them, as well as Verschoyle Court, between Stephen's Lane and Verschoyle Place, and Verschoyle House, between Verschoyle Place and Mount Street Lower in the Dublin 2 part of the Fitzwilliam/Pembroke Estate.

7

INCIDENTS, ACCIDENTS AND CRIME

Incidents can be interesting, funny or tragic. Accidents are always tragic for those who suffer them.

In modern newspeak, 'accidents' have been phased out; there are only 'incidents' now, including tragic and lethal ones. Incidents in the Dodder (or Donnybrook River) have been included in this chapter when the report makes it clear that people, animal or goods have been swept through Sandymount.

This list records some of the accidents and incidents reported in newspapers and other reports.

6 MAY 1665

The Intelligencer, 15 May 1665:

> We have here upon the Strand several races; but the most remarkable was by the Ringsend Coaches (Which is an odde kind of carre, and generally used in the countrye). There were a matter of twenty-five of them, and His Excellency the Lord Deputy bestowed a piece of plate upon him that won the race, and the second, third and fourth were rewarded with money. It is a new institution, and likely to become an annual custom; For the humour of it gives much satisfaction, there being at least 5,000 spectators.

The race most likely went from Ringsend down past Irishtown into what later became Sandymount. The Lord Deputy was Thomas, Earl of Ossory, the son of the Duke of Ormond who was Lord Lieutenant then and whom his son represented.

29 NOVEMBER 1729

Dublin Intelligencer:

> The late frequent rains here have caused much greater floods than are ordinary in the foords on the great roads leading to this city; but we have no word of damage caus'd thereby except the drowning of a few young cattle this week, which were bound on carriages to the Pass at Donnybrooke but were by a sudden rise of the waters borne down the river and drowned. The attendants very narrowly escaped.

7 FEBRUARY 1758

Dublin Gazette:

> We hear that the Right Honbl. Lord Fitzwilliam has given orders for 1,000 yards of cloths to be bought in this city, and distributed among the poor of both sexes on his Lordship's estate, a noble example! – and worthy of imitation by the great and opulent.

16 OCTOBER 1761

Sleator's Public Gazetteer, 17 October 1761:

> At night (Sunday) two men in a chaise and their driver were drowned in attempting to pass the Donnybrook River. The carriage was found near Ringsend.

4 AUGUST 1764

Sleator's Public Gazetteer, 7 August 1764

Saturday morning the 4th, was unfortunately drowned as he was bathing near Rings End, John Bury, Esq., who succeeded to a considerable estate on the death of his uncle, the Earl of Charleville.

29 DECEMBER 1791

Rev. Peter Richard Clinch, the first Roman Catholic Parish Priest of the parish of Irishtown and Donnybrook, died after he received an accidental blow by a boat oar which broke his jaw. He was only 29 years old. He is buried in the churchyard of St Matthew's in Ringsend.

Fr Peter Clinch was only in office for five years; he was respected and honoured by Catholics and Protestants. His gravestone inscription is, 'To the memory of the Rev. Peter Richard Clinch, Roman Catholic Pastor of this Parish, who died on the 29th Dec, 1791, in the 29th year of his age, and the fifth of his mission.'

19 OCTOBER 1807

Donnybrook Parish Register:

Sandymount, 19th October, 1807. I certify that I did this day, at one o'clock in the afternoon, marry Doctor Patrick Duigenan to Mrs. Esther Hepenstal, widow, at Sandymount, in the parish of Donnybrook, and county of Dublin, in the presence of the Rt. Honble. John Monck Mason and sundry other persons. Chars. Dublin [Earl of Normanton].

Patrick Duigenan, LL.D, MP was a Fellow of Trinity, had voted for the Union and was strictly against Catholic Emancipation, even though he had married a Catholic and had built a chapel for her in his house. Mrs Esther Hepenstal, *née* Watson, was his second wife.

22 MARCH 1808

Gentlemen's Magazine, 1808, Part 1, p. 274:

> Died 22nd March, the Revd. Dr. Hayes of Baggot Street, Dublin. Having dined in company with a friend at Black Rock, near Dublin, on his way home he unluckily took the Strand as the course by which to return. Being dark at the time, and the tide coming in, he mistook the usual route and passed over, swimming his horse great part of the way, to the Battery at the Pigeon House, where he and his horse became victims to his much regretted imprudence.

AUTUMN 1834

One of the first runs of the Dublin & Kingstown Railway was by invitation only; it was meant to show important personages the advantages and comfort of this new transport medium. A young fellow bet his friends that he would be on this trip without invitation. He actually managed to jump from a bridge onto the roof of a carriage. He also managed to hold on until the terminus was reached, even going through tunnels. What he had not reckoned with was the soot in the smoke. At the end of the line, he was discovered. Some of the illustrious personages who had been invited on this trip congratulated him for his initiative and courage, but none of them shook hands as he was nearly pitch black. It is said that he had to throw away the clothes he had been wearing and that it took him weeks to get the soot out of his hair and every wrinkle of his skin.

29 SEPTEMBER 1864

The Irish Times, 5 October:

> Two brothers aged respectively twenty and twelve years, sons of Edward S. Clarke, Esq., M.D., were drowned on 29th September while attempting to cross from the 'Shelly Bank' to Merrion.

1840s

A story is told about how a curate from Irishtown went home late at night from a sick call sometime before the building of the Star of the Sea Church in Sandymount. On his way, he saw very many cats mewing and growling, all of them heading in the same direction. He was tired and did not think much of the incident. The following morning, people in the neighbourhood talked about having been terrified by awful noises during the night. They then discovered that the area of the 'Waxies' Dargle' opposite the eastern end of Church Avenue was covered with hundreds of dead cats from all over the country. One of them wore a collar with the name and address of a lady in County Galway. It is said that six carts of Haig's Distillery were used to remove the dead cats. There never was an explanation for what had happened.

THE MID-TWENTIETH CENTURY

At some stage, the Sisters of St John the Evangelist urgently needed a water butt. At that time, the warden of the sisters was a monk of the Anglican Community of the Resurrection (CR). He happened to have some cousins in business at St James's Gate, so he went to ask them for a water butt. His cousins acknowledged him as a family member and the water butt was duly delivered and installed. The warden's name was Fr Jack Guinness.

TWENTY-FIRST CENTURY

Level Crossings
Many accidents nowadays are traffic accidents, but luckily
not many result in serious injuries to people. Accidents at
level crossings can be annoying, especially at Merrion Gates,
where, just to give one example, in December 2015 a lorry
with a trailer ignored the red warning lights and went across
the level crossing while the barriers were closing. The lorry
itself managed to pass over the level crossing, but one of the
barriers was caught between lorry and trailer and, as the driver
had not noticed this and had driven on, the barrier was bent
and damaged. This not only caused delays on the railway line,
but also on Rock Road and Strand Road.

Snow
The rare instances of snow on the roads in Sandymount can
play havoc with traffic as Irish drivers do not have much
experience of snow. In one instance, this resulted in a rather
comic incident, though it could have had bad consequences.
On a frosty day, all of the streets in Sandymount were covered
with snow which had been pressed and smoothed down by
cars driving over it. A car came down Newbridge Avenue.
The driver intended to turn into Sandymount Road. He turned
the steering wheel and braked at the same time. His car reacted
with a neat pirouette of 360° on the spot and then stopped.
The driver got out, scratched his head, went around the car,
looked at it from all sides, climbed back into it and drove on
carefully. Luckily there was no other vehicle on the road at
the time.

Incidents on the Strand
Any coastal village will know about tragedies or near-tragedies
at sea.

Sandymount has been lucky in that there have not been
any fatal accidents lately. Loss of property is another matter,
though. Some years ago, when it was still possible to drive
onto Sandymount Strand at Merrion Gates, one car per year

was lost, on average. People drove their car across Cock Lake onto a firm sandbank and then left it so late to go back that Cock Lake had become too deep to drive through it. The driver could get back to the strand but had to abandon the car, which had usually disappeared by next low tide.

Fog is another danger. During the summer of 2014, three teenage girls were surprised by a sudden sea fog while walking on Sandymount Strand. The girls became disorientated when visibility dropped to 100 metres and they found themselves surrounded by water. Luckily they could ring for help and, even more luckily, the crew of the Dún Laoghaire lifeboat managed to find them.

During the last few years, there has been more than one incident of people becoming stranded on a sandbank because they did not realise that the incoming tide had turned the sandbank into an island with rather deep water all around. In summer 2015, a couple and their dog in this situation were noticed by the helicopter of the Garda Air Support Unit as it flew over Sandymount Strand. The Gardaí alerted the Irish Coast Guard, who sent another helicopter. The Dún Laoghaire lifeboat was launched as well. The Garda helicopter landed on the sandbank and picked up one of the two people. The Coast Guard helicopter winched up the second person and their dog.

CRIME AND LEGAL ISSUES

Sandymount was situated between the highwaymen's meeting point at Beggars' Bush in the north and the Rock Road, notorious for robberies, in the south, so its residents rarely ventured out after dark unless armed at least until the end of the nineteenth century. Still, crimes did happen.

1348

> William Fitzwilliam (*c1325) was in 1348 pardoned by King Edward III of 'all transgressions and murders he had or might have committed in the exercise of Martial Law upon the Irish who bordered on The Pale'.

1666
Archdall's revised *Lodge's Peerage of Ireland*, vol. iv:

> His majesty's patent, bearing date 8th June 1664, and containing a gracious pardon to the Earl of Tyrconnel for all crimes, treasons, &c. committed before the 29th December 1660 in relation to any war in England and Ireland, and a clause of restitution to his estate, having been confirmed, he passed patent accordingly, 11th July 1666, for Ringsend, Merrion, &c.; and that year made a settlement thereof to the use of himself and his Countess Eleanor, for their respective lives; remainder to their heirs male; remainder to his brother William for life; remainder to Thomas, son of the said William, and his heirs male; with other remainders over.

Oliver, 2nd Viscount Fitzwilliam and Earl of Tyrconnel provided that his heirs could not suddenly lose the estate because somebody pointed out that they were heirs of a man who had co-operated with Cromwell before supporting the Crown again.

11 October 1729
Dublin Intelligencer:

> Portmarnock Man of War is come in from her cruise, without having the good fortune to meet with the pyrate she went in quest of.

With Beggars' Bush and the Rock Road infested by robbers and highwaymen, the sea obviously did not provide a safe route either.

17 December 1794
Anthologia Hibernica, iv p. 477:

> Last Wednesday night [17 December] the home of Lady Barry, of Sandymount, near Ballsbridge, was broken into by a gang of miscreants, and robbed of valuable articles to a considerable amount. These savage ruffians, on entering into

Lady Barry's chamber, fired a pistol at her, which fortunately missed its aim, but strewed the room with the slugs with which it was loaded.

This must have been happening in one of the new residences for which Viscount Fitzwilliam had hoped but it is not known which. Roslyn Park was there already, but inhabited by William Ashford; Tritonville Lodge was only built in 1796.

1807

The place where the following incident happened is officially just outside the borders of even the extended village of Sandymount as it is west of the railway, but it is near enough and the story is too good to be left out.

According to Weston St John Joyce, the Coach and Horses was situated just opposite the Merrion Gates. One night in 1807, ten highwaymen got into this inn and took all the landlord's cash, which amounted to £60 (over €6,200 in today's money). 'They then adjourned to the bar parlour, where they remained for about an hour drinking, and the health of the host was proposed and drunk with much enthusiasm, after which the unbidden guests departed with many apologies for their intrusion.'

Perhaps the tourist industry should use this story to illustrate how considerate and kind Irish people are – even robbers show extreme politeness.

21 April 1826
Dublin Morning Post, 22 April:

Yesterday morning, 21st April, between two and three o'clock, a murder, under most extraordinary and mysterious circumstances, was committed on the body of the Revd. George Wogan, curate of Donnybrook, in his house, in the place called by himself Spafield Place, situated off Sandymount Avenue, on the Blackrock Road; – four houses, which can be fully seen from the Rock Road, which the Revd. Gentleman who was a minister of the Established Church, purchased some time ago from the late Mr. Hodges of Sackville Street, and in one at the Western extremity of the row, he resided. – The report of this murder having created a very great sensation in the town, as soon as it was known, the Lord Mayor (Alderman Thomas Abbot) and Sheriff Alley with Sir Garret Neville, Police Magistrate of that division, accompanied the Coroner (Alderman Montgomery) and several very respectable citizens, went out before two o'clock to investigate on the spot this horrible transaction. What makes this horrible murder the more extraordinary is the fact that there was some valuable property in the house, but nothing was taken. The Reverend Gentleman had himself at the time of his death, a ring on the little finger of each hand; in the one on his left a beautiful cameo was set, which we understand he often said he would not give for £50; the other was a plain gold ring; - The Reverend Gentleman bore an excellent character in his neighbourhood and was, we understand, much beloved by the poor. He was between 60 and 70 years of age; about 5 ft. 8 in. in height, of a very athletic form, and not, for his time of life, at all infirm. He was a native of Cashel in the County of Tipperary but had lived between 30 and 40 years in the Diocese of Dublin.

Revd Beaver H. Blacker adds:

> Denis Hynes and George Stanley, both of Booterstown, having received sentence of death for a highway robbery committed the same night on the Blackrock-road, confessed the murder and were hanged.

1830s

It is well known that Robert Haig, the owner of the Dodderbank Distillery in Sandymount, had many encounters with revenue which are said to have developed into a kind of warfare, at least on his side. Some reports hold that the distillery was infamous for its nightly distilling and it was rumoured that some unpopular revenue officials who visited the distillery were never seen again.

6 September 1852

William Bourke Kirwan, a miniature painter, born in Dublin in around 1814, worked as an anatomical draughtsman for surgeons and as a picture cleaner. Around 1840, he exhibited miniatures and watercolours in the RHA. In 1852, he became known because of a trial in which he was accused of murdering his wife shortly after this lady had heard that her husband 'maintained an establishment at Sandymount, where he had a mistress by whom he had eight children'.

The court heard that one sunny day William Kirwan and his wife went to Ireland's Eye, he to paint in solitude, she to bathe in a cove as she was an ardent swimmer. When the sun had set, Kirwan and the hired boatman went to look for Kirwan's wife. The boatman found her dead. Some witnesses said they had heard the cries of a woman in distress.

Isaac Butt, QC, as Council for Defence, pointed out that the circumstances were not conclusive enough to condemn Kirwan. The cries the witnesses had heard could have been cries of seagulls. There were no witnesses of the deed and the medical evidence was not conclusive either. The jury could not agree on a verdict, but the judge threatened to keep them in court without food and drink, even overnight, until they had reached a conclusion. When asked by them about the observations of the medical witnesses, he recounted their testimonies from memory. After conferring for another fifteen minutes, the jury found Kirwan guilty. He was condemned to death by hanging.

As there still were doubts, Kirwan hired another solicitor. Finally, the sentence was commuted to transportation for life. Kirwan spent six years in a prison camp on Bermuda and, when that camp was closed, was brought back to Spike Island in Cork. He is said to have been freed around 1900 and is supposed to have died in America.

26 September 2010

In autumn 2010, Sandymount sadly became the location of the first reported road rage incident with fatal consequences in Ireland.

The incident occurred at the junction of Tritonville Road and Sandymount Road, where one driver tailgated another because he thought the other was driving too slowly. At some stage, both cars stopped, the drivers got out and shouted at each other. Back in their cars, the first one wanted to drive off but the second drove around him and forced him aside. This enraged the first driver, who took a hurley from the boot and started hitting the other's car. The driver then got out and was hit with the hurley on his arms and head, even after he had fallen to the ground. After the attack, the man who had been hit by the hurley managed to get into his car and drive home. The next day he felt nauseous; he was taken to St Vincent's Hospital by ambulance, then transferred to the head trauma unit in Beaumont Hospital, where he died three days later. The attacker admitted to manslaughter and was sentenced to twelve years' imprisonment, which on appeal was reduced to ten years.

8

DID YOU KNOW?

Martello towers were called after the sixteenth-century Torra di Mortella (Myrtle Tower) in Corsica, which impressed the British navy by its resistance against their attacks in 1794.

'W↑D', inscribed on the stone in front of the landside of the Martello tower, stands for 'War Department', the owner of the tower and some land around it. 'No2' means that this is border stone no. 2 (the equivalent stones nos 1 and 3 were lost with the building of the Promenade). '33FT11IN' indicates the distance to the actual border and 'West' gives the direction to this border. Stones like that were used when it would not be possible to put them at the actual border of the property of the War Department. In this case, that would have been the middle of St John's Road at the mini-roundabout.

On the first Ordnance Survey map of 1837, only Seafort Avenue and Sandymount Lane (now Sandymount Avenue) were named in the core village and Bath Avenue, Tritonville Road and Sydney Parade in the extended village.

The dragon on the chimney of the vestry for St John's church should be a wyvern as the crest of the Herbert family is a wyvern and not a dragon. The difference between a dragon and a wyvern is that a dragon has four legs and two wings and breathes fire. A wyvern also has two wings but only two legs. It might have a poisonous bite, but it cannot breathe fire.

Sidney Herbert, who was twice Secretary of State for War in the British Empire, was half Russian. His mother Katarina Vorontsova was the daughter of Count Semyon Romanovich Vorontsov, the Russian Ambassador at the Court of St James'.

The first headmaster of Sandymount National School earned £38 per annum (€5,400 in today's money).

The family name Doyle ('*Dubhghaill*' in Irish) means 'the dark stranger'; in other words, the Danish Viking. It is the second most common name in this area, after Byrne, whereas it is only the twelfth most common name in other parts of Ireland. That so many Doyles and Byrnes survived must mean that Vikings and Irish came to an arrangement in this area.

The idea of having a special symbol for goods made in Ireland was first aired at the beginning of the twentieth century. The design was a white 'e' in Celtic script which had the inscription '*Déanta in Éirinn*' in the 'e' and some Celtic ornaments in the spaces of the letter. It was introduced in 1906 to support native craftspeople and products. Christ Church, Sandymount Green, shows this symbol on a stained-glass window created by A.E. Child. Any time this symbol was granted, the grant was recorded with a number. A.E. Child's window has the number 27.

The Methodist Congregation of Sandymount ran a soup kitchen during the Second World War. Revd Dudley Levistone Cooney mentions in the *Dublin Historical Record*, Vol. 68, No. 2, Autumn/Winter 2015, that the Methodists in Sandymount became aware of the hardship suffered by the poorer residents of Sandymount and Ringsend during the war (officially 'The Emergency') and therefore opened a 'soup kitchen' from which meals were distributed. They did not get any help from State or city, only from the Red Cross. The work was voluntarily done and most of the cost was carried by the Methodist congregation of 250 people.

The tram no. 18 was called 'The Cross Line' because it crossed, shared tracks or met ten other lines.

The same tramline no. 18 also was called 'The Directors' Line' as it was said that its route had been chosen so that it went past the residences of many of the tram company directors to facilitate their wives' visits to each other.

Bus line no. 18 is one of the few Dublin bus lines that do not go into or through city centre but around it.

The Cordyline, a common tree in Sandymount and known as the 'Cabbage Palm', is not a palm tree at all. This native of New Zealand is a near relation of the American yucca and a distant relation of asparagus.

The Irish Times of Monday, 15 August 2011, mentioned a 'poetic competition' that the same paper had organised in 1887, asking their lady readers (only the ladies) to write a poem in praise of the golden jubilee of Queen Victoria. Augusta H. Lover, of 21 Sandymount Green, won with a poem that started:

> Hark! An anthem slowly swelling
> Echoes far o'er land and sea,
> Tis a year of joy and gladness,
> Tis Victoria's jubilee ...

Brauhaus Zeche Jacobi – Ärwin's Brauhaus GmbH in Oberhausen, Germany, still brews 'Mulvany's Dunkel', a dark beer called after William Thomas Mulvany from Sandymount.

BIBLIOGRAPHY

Ball, Francis Elrington, *A History of the County Dublin, Part the Second* (Dublin: Alex. Thom & Co Ltd, 1903).

Blacker, Revd Beaver H., *Brief Sketches of the Parishes of Booterstown and Donnybrook, in the County of Dublin* (Dublin: George Herbert, 1860).

Bolton, Jason, Tim Carey, Rob Goodbody and Gerry Clabby, *The Martello Towers of Dublin* (Dublin: Dún Laoghaire-Rathdown County Council and Fingal County Council, 2012).

Corcoran, Michael, *Through Streets Broad & Narrow – A History of Dublin Trams* (Leicester: Midland Publishing, 2000).

D'Alton, John, *The History of the County of Dublin* (Dublin: Hodges and Smith, 1838).

De Courcy, J.W., *The Liffey in Dublin* (Dublin: Gill & Macmillan, 1996).

Donnelly, The Most Revd Nicholas, *Short Histories of Dublin Parishes* (Dublin: Catholic Truth Society of Ireland, 1907).

Joyce, Weston St John, *The Neighbourhood of Dublin* (Dublin: M.H. Gill & Son Ltd, 1939).

Lewis, Samuel, *The Topographical Dictionary of Ireland* (London: S. Lewis & Co., 1837).

McKenna, Denis (ed.), *The Social and Natural History of Sandymount, Irishtown, Ringsend* (Dublin: Sandymount Community Services Publications, 1993).

McKenna, Denis (ed.), *The Roads to Sandymount, Irishtown, Ringsend* (Dublin: Sandymount Community Services Publications, 1996).

Murray, K.A., *Ireland's First Railway* (Swords, Co. Dublin: Irish Railway Record Society, 1981).

Ó Maitiú, Séamas, *Dublin's Suburban Towns 1834–1930* (Dublin: Four Courts Press Ltd, 2003).

Vocational Education Committee, *The Old Township of Pembroke City of Dublin* (Dublin, 2011).